CONCILIUM

concilium 1997/4

RELIGION AS A SOURCE OF VIOLENCE

Edited by

Wim Beuken and
Karl-Josef Kuschel

SCM Press · London
Orbis Books · Maryknoll

Published by SCM Press Ltd, 9–17 St Albans Place, London N1
and by Orbis Books, Maryknoll, NY 10545

Copyright © Stichting Concilium

English translations © 1997 SCM Press Ltd and Orbis Books, Maryknoll

ISBN: 0 334 03045 5 (UK)
ISBN: 1 57075 129 3 (USA)

Typeset at The Spartan Press Ltd, Lymington, Hants
Printed by Biddles Ltd, Guildford and King's Lynn

Concilium: Published February, April, June, October, December.

Contents

Introduction

Not all violence in this world has a religious basis, but far too much violence takes place in the name of a religion. Day by day reports come in: terror in the name of Islam; bombings by Catholics and Protestants; massacres by Hindus and Buddhists; genocide in Africa; war between Catholics, Orthodox and Muslims; violations of social justice in Latin America. The terror is usually enormous. Are religions still capable of inspiring people to use force, of legitimating violence and death?

There is no mistaking the fact that with the ending of the Cold War and the confrontation between East and West the last decade has brought political revolutions which were thought impossible. However, it has also brought a surprising growth in violence which is conditioned by religion. Ethnic, national and social conflicts have erupted in all parts of the world, in each of which religion plays a pernicious role. Conflicts are also increasing in which religion is the direct source of violence.

These problems, some of which are age-old and some of which are new, need to be understood; we need to grasp their anthropological, social, cultural and ethnological presuppositions. In this issue we seek to offer background information which will provide some orientation. We want to confront readers with scenes of violence and the targets at which they are aimed and at the same time lead them to feel that violence in the name of religion is neither natural nor unavoidable. On the contrary, in the articles which follow we want not only to give information about religion as a source of violence in various parts of the world and those towards whom it was directed, but also to show that violent scenarios are being overcome in the name of a religion which is understood and practised in a different way.

We deliberately want to avoid any religious enthusiasm by showing that in particular forms and style violence is an anthropological constant. It plays an important role – whether positively or negatively – in all the great religions. Rituals which recall violence are inherent in religions. Violence cannot simply be ingored, and naively denied. It is part of human life. But at the same time we need to see through the destructive elements which are immanent in violence, to transform them and overcome them. We want to show that religion can be the deep foundation of an ethic of the overcoming of violence. And at the end, for all our understanding, will come a firm no to violence, particularly to forms of violence within religions and within the church which are more subtle than death and terror.

By way of documentation we have included a bibliographical survey of the topic, in the form of an article by Edward Schillebeeckx, given at a symposium in his honour in the University of Tübingen in 1997. Edward Schillebeeckx here shows a lively sense of the upheavals of the time and at the same time attempts to indicate a way out of the crisis of the phenomena of violence. This seems to us to be significant for theological politics. In including this article we also show our respect for the lifelong contribution of this resolute Catholic theologian of reform, who as a founder of *Concilium* has particularly close ties to us.

Wim Beuken
Karl-Josef Kuschel

The Cult of Violence in the Name of Religion: A Panorama

François Houtart

Every society is violent. The violence can be physical or symbolic. It can be accepted or suffered. It appears in the construction, reproduction or transformation of social relationships. Since the appearance of the state, the state has built itself upon violence and Max Weber asserted that the exercise of legitimate violence is one of the characteristics of the state. There are those who say that the fundamental reason for this must be sought in the human heart. That is what Eugene Drewermann affirmed in his work on this topic.[1] Here I shall concentrate on the social questions. So the question is: what are the links between religion and violence?

It is too easy in an apologetic concern to claim that the content of the religions is essentially non-violent and that it is human beings who, whether individually or collectively, divert them from their meaning. In fact the roots of violence can be found right back in the religious, and that is why the religions can also easily serve as vehicles for violent tendencies. Here is a brief reminder of some of their features.

The sacrificial element is central to most religions. The theories of René Girard are well-known. He draws attention to the fundamental nature of violence[2] and the role of the sacrifice as a means of escaping from violence. Here sacrifice becomes increasingly ritual, issuing in symbolic violence. This gives it a more abstract form, as other authors claim in connection with the Vedic rites, provided that it does not lose the main effect of what is performed by the ideal offering, in which the one who sacrifices is himself the victim.[3] The sacralization of violence makes it possible to distinguish this latter from lawless violence,[4] which is rejected. Clearly all this can also be found in contemporary events, like the fact that the Algerian GIA cut the throats of their victims and decapitate them.

The struggle between good and evil is another source of violence very closely linked to religion. It is largely present in the Bible, in both the Old and New Testaments. Here I refer only to the book of Revelation. Identification with the good has justified much violence in the history of all the religions, from wars to colonial conquests, through internal repression of heretics and the Inquisition.

Finally, religious expansion has also been linked with the use of violence. The dozens of papal bulls accompanying the Portuguese mercantile enterprises of Henry the Navigator in Africa authorized him to conquer, dominate politically and reduce to slavery the people he met on his voyages to convert and combat the infidel. As for Latin America, the violence with which it was evangelized is known well enough.

If we touch on the great religious systems one after another we find the same traces. The basic texts reflect the ritualized violence of sacrifices, the use of violence for a superior good, and the need for violence in defence of the faith, along with the ethical regulation of non-legitimate violence, all aimed at ultimate peace.

Thus Hinduism is far from capable of being reduced to *ahimsa* (not causing evil, which is usually translated 'non-violence'), as is sometimes believed. The Rig Vedas offer different perspectives, notably in connection with sacrifice.[5] The kings call on the gods to give them victory, and the Bhagavadgita asserts that it is legitimate to kill in war, since the soul is immortal.[6] The Law of Manu establishes a hierarchy in which the Brahman, ontologically situated at the top of the scale of castes, is easily justified in the violent defence of its position, which has been obtained by the excellence of its former ways. Furthermore, to kill a brahman is not the same as to kill an untouchable (present-day dalit).[7] In the ambivalent pantheon of Hinduism we find a prominent place given to Kali, the goddess of destruction. As to the defence of the Hindutva, it finds political expression today above all in the BJP (Barattya Janaty Party), whose recent history shows that non-violence is not its cup of tea.

Buddhism has the best reputation, since it attaches more importance to *ahimsa* and the central virtue of compassion. In discussions of ethics, Buddhism emphasizes intention. Responding with violence to other violence is therefore not ruled out, though violence is not actually sought.[8] Islam is no exception and, putting more emphasis on justice than on love, as Ali Mazrui points out,[9] it offers little resistance to the tendency of certain groups to appeal to the attributes of this justice in their use of violence.

As for Judaism, André Wénin tells us: 'Nothing of human violence is absent from the Bible. Or rather, God is constantly involved in it, and often as an agent.'[10] Violence is particularly rife in times of messianic expectation. Does not the book of Exodus say that the Lord is a warrior (Ex. 15.3) and that divine interventions caused terrible destruction?

Christianity, basing itself on the same sources, has handed on the same religious culture, not hesitating to launch holy wars and crusades, drawing inspiration from messianic currents which were all the more violent since they were the expression of oppressed groups.

I. The contemporary conflicts

It was necessary to emphasize the internal source of possible violence at the beginning of religions in order to make it possible to understand the social functions which religion can take on in present-day conflicts. It would take too long to mention all of these conflicts. Reference to just some of them and their characteristics must suffice. In Asia, the case of Sri Lanka is striking for its cruelty; here two identities are in confrontation, one Sinhalese and Buddhist and the other Tamil and nationalist. India is in the grips of a twofold conflict, between fundamentalist Hindus and Muslims on the one hand and between superior castes and dalits (untouchables) who define themselves as oppressed on the other. In Africa, Algeria offers the everyday spectacle of killings in the name of religious orthodoxy, while in Rwanda, where religion as such is not at stake, some of the Catholic clergy have been seriously implicated in the massacres. In the Middle East, terrorism on both sides is justified by religious fidelity, whether to Israel or to Islam. In Latin America, even if guerrilla activity has subsided to some degree, violence is probably not extinct and there is a religious basis to certain struggles waged by the oppressed against the violence of the rich. In Europe, events in Ireland are interpreted as hostilities between Catholics and Protestants, when account is not taken of the colonial character of a struggle which has been going on for several centuries. As for former Yugoslavia, the threefold religious identity of the parties and the conflict sometimes recalls the wars of religion; the recognition by the Holy See, before any other European power, of Croatia and Slovenia has hardly clarified matters. One could quote many other examples here.

The situation is so striking that some observers have not hesitated to say, with Samuel Huntington, that future conflicts will prove to be between the West and the Islamic/Confucian states. He does not dare to speak of wars of religion and talks in terms of conflicts of civilizations.[11] How then are we to interpret all these situations?

II. Religion and social violence

Three main mechanisms seem to play a part in the association between religion and violence in the functioning of societies: the religious reading of social relationships, religion as a factor of identity, and the ethical legitimation or delegitimation of particular social relationships.

1. The religious reading of social relationships

This, strictly speaking, is the ideological function of religion, when it forms the cement of society by providing both a reading of social relationships and, by virtue of that, their legitimation. So this is a religious representation of the social order. The social order is willed by God, and the relations which exist between the social groups forming society are the fruit of a supernatural will. That usually passes for a kind of naturalization of the social order, nature and its laws being the fruit of divine creation. No one can touch them. Thus as late as the Medellin conference in 1968 a Brazilian bishop declared that he was excommunicating the peasants of his diocese who dared to accept land in the agrarian reform, since the right of property was of divine origin, and even the church did not have the right to alter it.

Such a position develops when it is necessary to justify relations of inequality which are not based on reciprocal services or regarded as such. That is why the whole feudal order based on the relationship between the lord (owner of land) and the peasant (without land) constructed its ideology on the divine order. Whereas such a position lost credibility in the West with the development of the mercantile classes and even more with industrial capitalism, something of it remained in the justification of power in societies marked by the Restoration, the right-wing dictatorships (Franco) and those of the transition between the populist nationalist Third World regimes (the Bandung era) and the penetration of international capitalism (Pinochet, Marcos, Suharto, Videla, Banzer, Mobutu, Somoza and many others).

Brahmanism is of the same type, naturalizing and spiritualizing the caste relationship. Despite the secularization of Indian society, the phenomenon remains powerful. Probably the progressive disappearance of this type of reading of social relationships is becoming an increasingly universal development as, for the collective conscience, the structure of society is recognized more clearly to be the work of human beings themselves. With the penetration of the market as a way of life and a form of organizing social relationships, other forms of ideology are replacing the religious reading: property justified by work, the laws of the market, etc.

Now any naturalization of unequal social relationships is a source of violence, whether in establishing them, reproducing them in time, or in the resistance which their transformation encounters. Apart from India – and again very partially – the relationship between violence and religion is no longer of this order.

2. *Religion as a cultural factor of identity*

Much nearer to us is the question of identity. This can be defined as the sense of belonging to a particular ethnic, national or social group which in return provides a certain social stability, a status, a view of the world, a way of thinking, in short a culture. At present religion can be one factor among others which define group identity. Group identity can be the result of an ethnic belonging which differs from others precisely by the fact of another religion.

That is the case in Sri Lanka, where the Sinhalese are Buddhists and the Tamils are Hindus. However, what is special in this case is that religion is invoked in only one of the groups, the Sinhalese. In fact the Sinhalese feel that their identity as a people is being attacked. They were converted to Buddhism in the time of the emperor Azoka. The Hindu Tamils gradually occupied the north of the island, thus destroying its cultural and religious unity. The use of the Tamils in the English colonial administration and their business skills gave them an influence all over the island, not just in the north. That provoked a nationalist reaction against them which erupted simultaneously with the reaction to British colonialism and at the moment of independence resulted in a refusal to recognize the basic rights of this minority. The identity defined by Buddhism is very solidly established and thus justifies an intransigent attitude and the pursuit of a merciless war. The Buddhist *sangha* sees this as a religious mission. Furthermore, a more political view of the conflict and the possibility of negotiation would represent a loss of power for the Buddhists. These two factors combine to make Buddhism a factor in the violence which is in direct contradiction to its basic philosophy.

In Ireland the question is different. English colonialism there has lasted for centuries and has twice subjected the Irish Catholics to real genocide. The settling of British colonists who became Anglicans added a religious accent to the economic and political dimension, and this is what public opinion remembers. It has to be said that cultural identity is expressed at the level of ethnic origin and of language, but above all of religion: on the one side for a people which for the most part has remained principally rural until now there are few of them left, and on the other for the colonists, in the minority, who are framed by their religious institutions. However, apart from these particular cases, the two religious institutions concerned have not claimed the role of standard-bearer in the struggles.

In Yugoslavia, the prime causes of the disintegraton of the nation were political and economic. Religious identity has played only a secondary role, but it has been a very serious and usually violent addition, one which has accentuated the conflict. The emphasis was in fact put on fidelity to one's own religious traditions and on the reconquest of territory thought necessary to the very existence of the group in its specific religious character. European geopolitics was also involved in this conflict: we might recall the dream of a belt of Catholic countries from the Baltic to the Adriatic as a bulwark against both Communism and Orthodoxy. This led the Holy See to display much tolerance towards the Fascist Croat regime which was allied with the Nazis and, later, to recognize the two new republics over-hastily. Serbia has aimed at a Slavonic and Orthodox solidarity, and many Islamicist fighters signed up with the Bosnian Muslim forces after service in the ranks of the Afghan Mujahaddin. It is true that some religious institutions have several times tried to act as moderators in the conflict, but that does not affect the social fact of identity through religion very much, or the rivalry which has become established between the respective religious authorities.

Beyond question, one of the most striking examples is that of the conflict between Israel and the Palestinians. The religious factor is relevant for only part of the two camps, but this is a numerically and socially important part. On both sides the religious argument is central. Each people has its own arguments, but each believes that it is acting in the name of God. For the Jewish extremists, the chosen people has to defend the land given to it by God: there are plenty of biblical references to which they can appeal for support. The use of force, and thus of violence, is a religious duty, not in itself, but to safeguard a superior value. For the Palestinians of Hamas, defence of Muslim identity is central and sacred. It is in fact the condition for salvation. In the name of Muslim identity violent methods are used as a defence against a group which has considerably more resources. Both sides kill in the name of God, and both do so in order that one day a real peace may be established, depending in the last resort on faithfulness to the religious aim.

When we get to Algeria (to which we could add similar situations, from Iran to Egypt and from the Sudan to Saudi Arabia), the question of identity is at the centre of the problem, but in yet another dimension. This time we have an identical reaction to the destruction of a culture and the economic and political failure of the modern Western approach. This reaction is shown both against the West, its economic model, its political institutions and imperialist manifestations, and against the Westernized local social class, the material foundations of its existence and the political forms which it has adopted. It is also held together by everything which is the symbolic expression of this situation, in particular in the sphere of mass communications, in customs of dress, above all for women, and in religion.

This struggle is being carried on specifically in the name of Islam, since Islam is the sole certain value in the face of the social disintegration of traditional societies, the loss of meaning in existence, and the introduction of new customs which lead to a loss of orientation. The extremist movements draw their recruits from among the most vulnerable groups in society, and in particular among the young people who have no future. They develop in pockets of piety, even if their leaders are often religious agents or fundamentalist intellectuals. The religious hardening is not shown by a war of religion against the other groups of believers. If violent acts have been committed against Christian religious figures, they do not demonstrate opposition to Christianity as such so much as opposition to what the presence of these figures represents, since they are associated with a satanized West.

The development in our day of these identical religious reactions may surprise us. People thought that it was a thing of the past. But these reactions are to be put on the same level as the ethnic or apparently ethnic explosions in Africa, in north-east India or among the Chiapas in Mexico, or yet again as the multiplication of conflicts among the castes in India, in particular the reaction of the dalits. In fact, paradoxical though it might seem, the extension of a capitalist market economy, necessarily inegalitarian and exploitative because of the very philosophy which it conveys, is reviving conflict based on precapitalist social relationships in peripheral societies.

Since the majority of the populations are not directly integrated into the wage structure (the relationship between capital and labour), but experience the effects of the world system indirectly, they express their frustrations and their protests in the forms which their cultures have handed down to them. That is why the policies of structural adjustment imposed by the World Bank and the International Monetary Fund can only reinforce these phenomena. Their short-term nature increases poverty; they abolish the networks of social protection, abolish food subsidies, and make access to education and health more difficult.

Samuel Huntington may perhaps be right to say that these are conflicts between civilizations, but his view is very limited, since he does not go further than appearances. The deepest causes are to be found at the level of the globalization of an economic system which reduces the whole of human reality to its own rationality and thus revives among those left out of account forms of conflict which are apparently traditional but in fact are created in advance by the system. In a certain number of cases the manifestations of violence will have a religious expression, and some of them will be fed by aspects intrinsic to the religions, as I demonstrated earlier. However, they are not a simple return to a nostalgic past, but rather a cultural reconstruction on the basis of available elements to cope with a very pressing situation.

3. Religious support for an ethic of social relationships

The situations to which I have alluded are very different from those in which religion served as a grid for reading social relationships and therefore also for legitimation. These are cases in which there is no sacralization of relationships but in which their functioning receives religious support. That can also associate religion directly or indirectly with violence. We may consider two contemporary cases which are diametrically opposed.

The first is the moral support given to the market economy which, according to the Nobel prize-winner Milton Friedman, is simply another name to denote the capitalist economy. We find such an ethical legitimation in the writings of Michael Novak, who sees the market as the form of organizing the economy which most corresponds with the gospel and the parameter of which is the American model.[12] It also recurs in what is said by Michael Camdessus, the director of the International Monetary Fund, who asserts that it is 'an economy of responsibility, in which human beings can employ all their dimensions'.[13] Its imperfections and abuses must be corrected, with sharing and gifts completing what the invisible hand of the market has not been able to accomplish. So there is complementarity here.

What these positions seem to ignore is the existence of unequal social relationships which do not put the partners in the market economy in a position of reciprocity. Moreover the market economy creates and reproduces inequalities by the very logic of its functioning. This is a logic which it tends to impose on a world scale and in every sector of human life, with virtually no counter-balance. The lack of attention to social relations makes the standpoints adopted very illusory. Supporters of the market economy can go on to say that the freedom of the market is the mother of all freedoms, whereas today we can see an increase in social divisions and poverty; market economies accommodate very well to anti-democratic regimes, policies which repress social movements, and structural violence in social relations.

The moral support given to the social struggle of the oppressed with religious arguments drawn from prophetic currents is quite different. This is not necessarily violent but is often so, and risks becoming so again in coming years after the physical, social and cultural ravages of neoliberal policies. We do not live in a non-violent mode, and Mgr Romero, archbishop of San Salvador, rightly said that it was necessary to distinguish between the violence of the powerful and that of the oppressed, even if he favoured non-violent means. That is the inevitable risk of an ethical commitment within social relations of exclusion and oppression.

I can conclude by saying that every consideration of the topic of religion and violence must include an analysis of all aspects of situations, both the function of religions in society and the social relationships which appear in them. Moral judgment cannot by-pass analysis.

Translated by John Bowden

Notes

1. Eugene Drewermann, *La spirale de la peur, le christianisme et la guerre*, Paris 1994.
2. René Girard, *Violence and the Sacred*, Baltimore 1979.
3. Denis Vidal, Gilles Rarabout and Eric Meyer, 'On the Concept of Violence and Non-Violence in Hinduism and Indian Society', *South Asia Research* 14.2, Autumn 1994, 201.
4. Ibid., 202.
5. Ibid.
6. Mark Juergenmeyer, 'The Terrorist who Longs for Peace', *The Fletcher Forum for World Affairs*, Winter/Spring 1996, 7.
7. Vidal et al., 'On the Concept of Violence' (n. 3), 208.
8. Juergenmeyer, 'The Terrorist who Longs for Peace' (n. 6), 7–8.
9. Quoted by Sohail H. Hashi, 'International Society and its Islamic Malcontents', *The Fletcher Forum on World Affairs*, Winter/Spring 1996, 23.
10. André Wénin, 'La Bible pour démasquer la violence', *Bulletin de Pax Christi, Bruxelles/Wallonie* 19,3, September 1996. The author adds that this presence of violence underlies another reflection, God's call to transform evil into life.
11. Samuel P. Huntington, 'The Clash of Civilizations?', *Foreign Affairs* no. 72, summer 1992, 22–49.
12. Michal Novak, *The Spirit of Democratic Capitalism*, Lanham, New York 1991.
13. Michael Camdessus, *Conférence sur le marché et la religion*, Notes et documents 44, September-December 1995, Institut Maritain, Rome.

I · Religion and Violence: Outbreak and Overcoming

Africa: Rwanda

Paul Nzacahayo

A. Outbreak

I. Introduction

Much has been published on the Rwandan tragedy that cost the lives of hundreds of thousands, if not millions, of innocent people. On searching for the roots of that tragedy some scholars went back as far as the sixteentnh century, with the first Hutu/Tutsi encounter on Rwandan soil and the beginning of Tutsi domination. Others started with the 1959 popular revolution and the violence that resulted in thousands of Tutsis being killed and others going into exile. Some began their investigations only with Habyarimana's regime, which was held responsible for the 1994 tragedy. Whilst these questions of history remain unresolved, there is also the question of why such violence in a religious society as Rwanda was possible: 62% are Roman Catholic, 18% are Protestant, 8% are Seventh Day Adventist, 1% are Muslim and the remaining 11% follow traditional religions. Rwanda is a country where Hutus (84% of the population), Tutsis (15%) and Pygmees (1%) speak the same language, live together in mixed communities throughout the country, marry each other,[1] partici-pate together in churches, schools, hospitals and invite each other to special ceremonial occasions.

Religious people have been accused of involvement in the massacres. There are even those who go as far to accuse the church of planning and promoting the violence. The purpose of the first part of this article is to contribute towards understanding the kind of violence we have suffered and what the role of religion has been in this. I intend to approach the topic in three ways. First, I shall seek an understanding of violence in general and in the Rwandan context in particular; few people have managed to hold all the different aspects together. Secondly, I shall examine the role of religion in the outbreak and continuation of that violence. Finally I shall assess where we (Rwandan people in general) got it wrong. The argument that runs through the article is that most people have been too busy accusing each other to recognize their own role in the tragedy.

II. Understanding violence

The *Collins Cobuild Dictionary of Essential English* defines violence as a 'behaviour which is intended to hurt or kill people, for example hitting or kicking or using guns or bombs'. Among various kinds of violence there is that of a political nature. Ted Honderich defines this as 'a considerable or destroying use of force against persons or things, a use of force prohibited by law, directed to a change in the policies, personnel or system of government, and hence also directed to changes in the existence of individuals in the society and perhaps other societies'.[2] Political violence can be used either for maintaining or disturbing the *status quo*. As far as individuals are concerned, Thomas Cullinan connects the 'violence within' each one of us to the 'violence without' each one of us. The former has to do with inner conflicts – our ego which holds us subservient to our immediate self-interests, slaves to our prejudice, to security, to our passions and, far more importantly, to fear. The latter is about our reactions to external social conflicts in our society. Cullinan argues that this outer violence can take three forms: 'hot' violence, by which he means guns, bombs; 'cold' violence, by which he means economic power to dominate or to destroy those who lack it; and 'cool' violence, which gives apparent legitimation both to the hot and to the cold.[3] At the very source of violence, we find all sorts of inequalities which have to do with economic, social and political life: inequalities in food, shelter, land, health, freedoms and lack of them, self-determination and demands for equality between peoples. It is in this respect that Paul Tournier suggests that occasionally violence can be justified to get rid of an unbearable situation.[4] The right or wrong use of violence leads us to consider the concept of the just war. Such an examination, however, is beyond my scope.

III. The slaughter of the innocents

History informs us that it was the Hutus who occupied the land of Rwanda after the pygmies. They organized the country into chiefdoms and each had its own chief. During the sixteenth century the Tutsis arrived. Then one class emerged from within the Tutsi race which began to dominate and oppress the other people. There started an endless violent struggle for power. Two weapons have been used, ethnicity and regionalism; the latter less than the former. The colonialist policy of divide and rule only exacerbated the tensions. They supported the oppressive Tutsi ruling class in the first place, but towards the end of the 1950s the scale tilted in favour of the new Hutu elite. The bloody revolution of 1959 left many people (Hutus and Tutsis) dead and forced the majority of the Tutsi ruling class into exile. The attempts of the Tutsi refugees to regain power by force during the 1960s made things worse, since each attack corresponded with all sorts of persecutions against the Tutsi community living inside the country. In 1973 ethnicity was less expressed than regionalism as a justification for the military coup. Members of the overthrown government were systematically murdered. Hutu killed Hutu.

Towards the end of the 1980s fear grew that the old oppressors (the Tutsis) were going to regain power. When the RPF (Rwandan Patriotic Front, the Tutsi-dominated rebel movement) launched a massive and decisive attack in October 1990, the Hutu authorities played a highly sensitive card which they knew would go down well with peoples: ethnicity. The RPF, which was fighting for power, was accused of seeking to restore the monarchy, to slaughter political and administrative authorities and Tutsis who refused to collaborate with them.[5] After three years of indoctrination and media poisoning,[6] people were already polarized. This is how in April 1994 some people inclined to the genocide ideology as the 'final solution' – the extermination of Tutsis and the opponents of the existing regime in order to solve the problem once and for all. The plan failed: the Tutsi community was not fully exterminated, nor were the political opponents done away with. Instead, this evil plan allowed the Tutsi-dominated rebels to gain power (in July 1994), after which there was no room for either bargaining or negotiations.[7] In the process Hutus killed not only Tutsis but also other Hutus. Tutsis killed Hutus as well.[8] When the RPF took power in July 1994, the new strong men in Kigali were even more frustrated and inclined to violence than ever before: most of them had lost their entire families. They were ruling a country full of orphans, widows and people with physical and psychological scars. The inevitable violence and oppression started again as a sort of revenge.[9] The recurring attacks of the militias and former army on Rwanda from Zaire made things worse. The vicious circle of violence went on. We have unfortunately reached the point of no return, where it is no longer clear who is killing whom and why.

The failure of the Western powers lay not only in not giving appropriate attention to the sharing of the cherished cake (power and all that goes with it) between Hutus and Tutsis, but also in ignoring and perpetuating the conflicts by supplying weapons to the warring factions.

Although the population explosion and economic problems were biting hard on the ordinary people, it would be wrong to suggest that these were at the source of the Rwandan violence. Although during the killings, people turned to the looting of victims' properties, Rwandans were economically better off than many other Africans. If economic problems are to be considered, then they should be discussed in terms of the powerful trying to monopolize the resources (education, land, employment and finance) to their advantage.

It is clear that the Rwandan conflict originates in the inner violence of the country's ruling authorities, sustained and fed by the colonialist policy of divide and rule. The existence of Hutus and Tutsis was an appropriate field for such a policy.

IV. The role of religion

First of all, both Christian missionaries and Muslims found on arrival a divided and troubled society, where both inner and outer violence was taking root in people's minds. But this seemed to be an opportunity for the gospel.

Secondly, Christianity has appeared to be dismissive of the traditional religion of Rwanda. One of the reasons the king of Rwanda was suspicious of the Christian missionaries was that he was afraid that they would contaminate his traditional religion, which he was bound to protect.[10] Traditional religion was based on a cult of sacred warrior-kingship which gave powerful legitimacy to the monarchy. The king's suspicions were well-founded as it became clear that some Christians understood their commitment to Jesus as a process of saving people (as quickly as they could and as many as possible), putting them into 'Noah's ark' before it was too late. To a certain extent Christian missionaries implemented this mission of making disciples by bullying men and women to abandon their cultural roots and become Christians overnight. There were also hostilities (though not open) between Roman Catholics and Protestants.

It is with this weakness that Christianity had to address the social inequalities and oppression present in Rwandan society. The church as an institution has been shifting its support from one side to the other following the movement of power; it has alternatively been seen as a Hutu church, then a Tutsi church, and finally a Hutu church again.[11] The church also missed so many opportunities to put things right.[12] As *African Rights* put it, 'the legacy of this identification lives on and has contributed enormously to the deep politicization of the church'.[13] In this way the church is part of the problem and has contributed to it. On the individual level, the challenge was how Christians were going to manage the dual identity in time of crisis. Two forces were in play here: on the one hand there was an ethnic ideology promoted by the politicians: and on the other, love and unity among Christians promoted by the gospel. Every time political violence erupted, Christians responded according to the categories of the outer violence described earlier: some reacted with 'hot' violence, with machetes, spears, guns, grenades and bombs;[14] others with 'cold' violence, by exercise of power in support of those involved in 'hot' violence; others with 'cool' violence, by giving apparent legitimation to both the 'hot' and the 'cold' violence. Some of us are to be found here.[15] When it was time to speak, we didn't speak; when the tragedy broke out, we ran for our lives.[16]

As far as Muslims are concerned, although some of the Qur'an scriptures (Sura 9, 74; 48, 27–28 and 9, 5) imply the use of violence and force to convert people to Islam, Islam has little to do with the political violence in Rwanda. The reason was that not only is it a minority religion (1% of the Rwandan population), but it did not reach into the countryside where 95% of the population live, and also did not engage much in social activities such as schools and hospitals.

V. Conclusion

The Rwandan case is a tragic example in which violence breeds violence. Christians killed other Christians for political reasons. Although the conduct of some churchmen has been questioned, it would be wrong to suggest that the church as an institution planned and implemented the genocide. On the whole the church is made up of criminals and victims, heroes and heroines.

We failed to recognize that we are naturally violent and that we fear not only violence from others but also violence from within ourselves; for it is always there underneath, and it might break out at any moment to ravage that all we hold dear. The lie that people have wanted to believe is that violence is wholly outside themselves and to see that as the cause of all their problems. Efforts and energies have been concentrated on demonizing the other and making him or her neurotic and hateful. Christians did not escape such pitfalls. First of all we have been on the defensive, trying to vindicate ourselves and our behaviour. Secondly, we have all succumbed to the temptation of pointing to the other as the source of the violence, and so have called for violent and drastic punitive measures: he or she must be given a lesson. Such an interpretation is inadequate and hides people from the ongoing and increasing violence from within – from the side that claims to be saint and saviour.

B. Overcoming

I. Introduction

Sometimes we think that if we exclude the violent person/group from our community things will be better. But this creates rather a false kind of security, since the person/group waits for the opportunity to fight back. At other times, we try to solve the problem by disempowering or silencing the violent person/group through oppression and persecution. This also does not work. Instead it makes the person more violent. These different ways have been tried by Rwandan politicians, but in vain. Violence only breeds violence.

I would argue that churches need a mature theology which relates to the reality of the people it addresses, but which is also imbedded in the grace and love of God. Some of the aspects religious people may be willing to look at in order to overcome violence include recogntiion of the offence, repentance, forgiveness, reconciliation and tolerance. In all aspects, religious people have to be vigilant: to anticipate the problems and create tomorrow by preparing people for whatever lies ahead.

II. Lessons from the past

Protestant Christians seemed to suggest: 'Face up to the personal *metanoia* and liberation in yourself, and public structural liberation and peace will follow automatically. Personal conversion first – everything else will look after itself.' Focussing on this alone brought about many misgivings. First of all it led to what Thomas Cullinan calls 'a subjective enthusiasm',[17] a sort of subjective piety that absorbs people with great vigour, but does not relate to the nature of their society or face the basic questions of the political realities they are in.

On the other hand the Roman Catholic Church has been trapped in a kind of morally political awareness, which wanted to be very relevant to the Rwandan society but was basically unrelated to the truth of God as revealed in Christ. Its involvement in politics was, by and large, characterized by taking sides with violent and brutal regimes so that even when it tried to speak for the voiceless, it was in a very weak position to do so. Some of the clergy moved far too close to the regime and forgot what God had called them for.[18] The Roman Catholic leadership was accused of collaborating too much with the government and its army.[19] The Roman Catholic attempts to address the problem of violence were deeply hampered by internal divisions and confusion.[20]

Church leaders argued it was not all bad: they organized public evangelistic teams and public preaching in stadiums and basic Christian communities, issued joint statements for their congregations, met the warring factions and called both Christians and non-Christians involved in the killings to stop.[21] Unfortunately many refused to listen.

The Muslims' record throughout the genocide has been positive (when violence erupted they held on together and protected each other).[22] It is not only that today many of them interpret *jihad* (struggle) in a spiritual manner (striving for the cause of God), but also that the minority always survive by protecting each other. This was facilitated by the fact that in Rwanda Muslims (Hutus and Tutsis) lived together in the *cités*. It was easy to put up blockades around their areas and prevent the militias from entering.

III. The heroes and heroines of the tragedy

Very recently, after I had given a talk about forgiveness in the light of the Rwandan context, a lady asked me whether there was persecution of Christians in Rwanda. My answer was yes and no, depending on what kind of Christian one wants to be. Father Sylivio Sindambiwe was killed in a very suspicious car accident after many death threats only because of his writings.[23] In fact, one of these death threats involved a basketful of human excrement that was thrown into his face by a stranger who entered his office in Kigali prior to his mysterious death. Israel Havugimana, former Area Secretary of the African Evangelistic Enterprise, was killed on the first night of the massacres only because of his outspoken sermons. There are many other examples of Christians who stood firm against evil. Among the clergy there were those who shepherded their flock like Fabien Nzabagurira (a local Pentecostal pastor) who saved many people either by organizing their escape, or by protecting them at the risk of his life and that of his family.[24] There are many other examples of this kind in all denominations.

Let me pay homage to these Christians and to the Muslims who have fought for a peaceful society. They have put their neighbours' lives above their ethnic allegiances, confronted conventional violence and accepted with fortitude the consequent abuse, persecution and death. They stood firm as heroes-heroines among so many of their colleagues who floated with the tide, trimming and altering their views to obtain popularity and other privileges. Death was impotent to intimidate them into violence.

IV. Towards a non-violent society

Paul Tournier points out that violence has to be invested in or transferred to an object if it is to be handled. He recalled an incident when he hurled his

Bible into the far corner of the room in the course of an argument with his wife. At other times we express our violence by banging the door behind us or thumping the table. This was also the case when in the early 1990s up and down the country huge forests were set on fire by angry mobs and we did not understand why. In December 1993, a Ugandan evangelist, commenting on how evil the human heart is, challenged us, asking whether these forests were Hutus or Tutsis.

Paul Tournier concludes that, since each act of violence is followed by vengeance and that vengeance calls for another, there is a need for a sacrifice, a sort of scapegoat that has to break the chain. Jesus is the one, says Paul Tournier, who by his death broke into the vicious circle of our violence, assuming it without paying it back.[25] It is only when we allow him to take this violence (through genuine repentance) that we can start the long process of reconciliation with God, with one another and with nature. Otherwise we, as Christians, will continue to deceive ourselves and mislead others: it is not that our religion is a false one, but that we fail to do what is required from us whilst claiming to be better than others. Some of us do this by holding on to the kind of Christianity that helps us to keep our consciences pure and not getting our hands dirty; others by letting political ideology overtake the gospel imperatives that should rule our actions. What does matter is that we engage in God's work and invite the Holy Spirit to be a permanent check on whether or not our engagement is pure as we go along. Then media, education and all other means can work together to promote a violence-free society.

V. Practical tips:

Whenever violence damages our relationships with one another and with God religious people should concentrate among others things, on:

(a) Recognition of the wrong that has to be done. This is a major breakthrough in the process of putting things right. It is an open recognition that our relationship both with our neighbours and with God has been broken or deeply affected by the course of action taken. There is little to expect from somebody who cannot even admit that he or she has done wrong. As humans we also have the natural plight of being sinful, weak and falling short of the glory of God.

(b) Repentance. If someone acknowledges the sin but does nothing about it, it makes no difference. He or she is just a cynic. Repentance points to the remorse of the offender, the genuine willingness to make amends and the determination not to commit the sin over again.[26] It points also to the grace and forgiving love of God. By repentance, our sinful nature and weaknesses are transformed into strength by the grace

and forgiving love of God that hold us together and give a meaning to our lives.

(c) Forgiveness. This double act involves God and the person that has been offended. An act of violence normally calls for a reaction of the same kind. In other cases, people prefer to keep violence within themselves, but only because of their physical weakness to hit back. Forgiveness means not only that they no longer see the crime committed as being on their offenders' head but also that they will not hit back and will not hold violence within themselves. As Neil noted, it is a 'let-go' of the burden and resentment against the wrongdoer.[27] This is why some psychologists hold that forgiveness has profound healing power, both psychologically and physically. One recent and powerful example is that of South Africa. Nelson Mandela and some of his colleagues won a political battle against those who were promoting the 'one white, one bullet policy'. These people held that in the new South Africa, Blacks would have to get rid of White fellow citizens. Michael Cassidy, writing about the South African experience, commented: 'That we had not gone over the edge was everywhere hailed as a miracle – the South African Miracle.'[28] Indeed God used people like Mandela and others to forgive and let go. Then reconciliation became the foundation for a new South Africa.

(d) Reconciliation. Derived from the Latin, reconciliation refers to 'to come together', 'to assemble', 'to walk together' or an act by which people who have been apart and split-off from one another begin to stroll or march together again.[29] As Hezkias pointed out, reconciliation contains four dimensions: reconciliation with God, reconciliation with the self, reconciliation with one's neighbours and the human community at large, and reconciliation with nature.[30] Two of these four dimensions tend to be minimized, if not ignored, in the process of reconciliation: reconciliation with the self that underlies the internal conflict with oneself but once achieved produces tranquillity, peace and harmony within individuals; reconciliation with nature that embraces our relationship with God's creation.[31]

(e) Toleration. This is to acknowledge that human beings are all different, physically, intellectually, and psychologically, and that human relations have to be characterized by a great sense of mutual respect. In this context, 'to tolerate' would mean to endure or put up with a person, identity, activity, idea or organization to which or whom one does not really subscribe.[32] People agree to disagree, live together with their differences (Blacks and Whites, Christians and non-Christians, Muslims and Hindus, Hutus and Tutsis, educated and uneducated, weak and strong, rich and poor, those with different opinions, and so on) without any attempts to dominate, exploit, discriminate or kill each other.

In places which have not yet experienced a great deal of violence, religious people might also consider these two points:

(a) Anticipate the dangers. Most Rwandans silently observed the country running towards the catastrophe. Despite all the signs, the majority of Christians were taken by surprise and seemed unprepared to deal with the tragedy. Little was done to prepare the population or the country for the impending destruction of the country.

(b) Do not just pray but also do something. Many people believe that not only did Christians not rise above their ethnic allegiances to put into practice the love of the neighbour, but also that there was little 'prophetic voice' to warn those struggling for power about the consequences of their actions on the nation as a whole.

VI. Conclusion

Our experience with violence has been a catalogue of failure: failure to share power and resources, the failure of Christians to appreciate that their faith is not about personal salvation abstracted from social realities and that liberation from outer violence cannot be achieved without addressing inner violence. Our big temptation was to overcome violence by violence. This did not pay off, and our response has been inappropriate. We are still struggling with internal divisions, physical and spiritual wounds. But the healing can occur when the members of the Christian community recognize their own violence, and then repent of it. This makes more sense since, as Paul Tournier argued, what makes Jesus our Saviour is that he takes our violence on himself, keeps it and does not pay it back. In his testimony Antoine Rutayisire said that he lost his father when he was only five; then, in 1983, he was fired from his job as a university lecturer on the grounds of ethnic equilibrium. But it was only when he gave up all the anger and violence inside him that he became completely healed: 'I was released and healed from inside and I no longer felt the gripping pang of bitterness whenever one of the old enemies was mentioned in my presence.'[33]

Notes

1. This intermarriage has been going on for centuries and has happened at all levels of Rwandan society, but more frequently among the elite and politicans. Kayibanda, who was the second president, is said to have had a Tutsi wife.
2. T. Honderich, *Violence for Equality*, London 1989, 8.
3. T. Cullinan, *The Passion of Political Love*, London 1987, 17, 21.
4. P. Tournier, *The Violence Inside*, London 1977, 67.

5. African Rights, *Rwanda, Death, Despair and Defiance*, London 1994, 64.

6. The importance of the mass media in whipping up popular sentiment cannot be underestimated. This was mainly done by RTLM, Radio Television Libre des Mules Collines, controlled by Hutu extremists; Radio Muhabura, controlled by the RPF (Rwandan Patriotic Front); Radio Rwanda (state controlled); and the newspapers which proliferated in the run-up to the catastrophe.

7. The Arusha peace agreements were then rendered invalid by the extremists, probably from both sides, who did not want to share power.

8. The massacre of thousands of Hutu refugees in Kibeho in May 1995, the massacres of Catholic bishops in Gitarama in June 1995 and the massacres of Hutus in Byumba are only a few examples.

9. Amnesty International has compiled its findings in a document called 'Rwanda – Alarming Resurgence of Killings'. It is about extrajudicial executions by the Rwandan Patriotic Army, extrajudicial executions of local officials and detainees, and deliberate and arbitrary killings by armed opposition groups. This document is dated August 1996.

10. I. Linden. *The Church and the Revolution*, Manchester 1977, 33.

11. Ibid., 73–74, 152–74, 249–72.

12. Most of the education system was in the hands of the church (both Roman Catholic and Protestant).

13. African Rights, *Rwanda. Death, Despair and Defiance* (n. 5), 9.

14. Christians killed other Christians; priests, pastors and bishops were killed by members of their congregations. Some Christians known for their faith and commitment to the gospel have been caught between the two ideologies – the RPF killing those it found unsupportive to its ideas (e.g. the bishops killed in Gitarama) and presidential guard militias killing those who criticized Habyarimana's regime (e.g. Israel Havugimana of the African Evangelistic Enterprise).

15. I was not in the country in April 1994 when the massacres started on a large scale. But I wonder what I should have done.

16. Almost all missionaries left when they were most needed. For a while they did succeed in closing their doors to the militias, who wanted to kill those they protected. Their white skin gave them an outstanding advantage that was useful during the first days of the tragedy. Then the situation went out of control and they, too, ran for their own lives.

17. T. Cullinan, *The Passion of Political Love*, London 1987, 31.

18. The former Roman Catholic archbishop has been strongly criticized for being a member of the single ruling party (MRND). No doubt the tone of the criticism would change if he had influenced the party positively.

19. A. Rutayisire, *Faith Under Fire. Testimonies of Christian Bravery*, London 1995, 115.

20. According to African Rights, the then Roman Catholic Archbishop Nsengiyumva waited ten days to raise his voice on the issue of the massacres. Even when he did that he did not condemn what was happening.

21. There were lots of sermons, documents and statements from the clergy and from church leaders in particular calling people to remain calm and not to give in to the evil plan.

22. T. Gatwa, 'Mission and Ethnicity in Rwanda: History and Perspective', a paper presented at a forum held in Edinburgh (June 1996) on mission and ethnicity.

23. African Rights, *Rwanda. Death, Despair and Defiance* (n. 4), 492.

24. Rutayisire, *Faith Under Fire* (n. 19), 88.

25. Tournier, *The Violence Inside* (n. 3), 76.

26. There are three possible outcomes for somebody who has committed an act of violence: (i) he/she denies it and obviously does not repent; (ii) he/she acknowledges it but cannot or does not want to amend it; or (iii) he/she acknowledges it and seeks to amend with a firm determination not commit it over again (though he/she may fail).

27. S. Neil, *A Genuinely Human Existence*, London 1959, 211.

28. M. Cassidy, *A Witness For Ever: The Dawning of Democracy in South Africa. Stories behind the Story*, London 1995, 5.

29. J. O. Nelson, *Dare to Reconcile: Seven Settings for Creative Community*, New York 1969, 16.

30. A. Hezkias, *Peace and Reconciliation as a Paradigm. A Philosophy of Peace and its Implications on Conflicts, Governance and Economic Growth in Africa*, Nairobi 1993, 9.

31. I referred earlier to the fact that violence is sometimes directed at objects. In the Rwandan case, not only forests have been set on fire, but also rivers have been contaminated with dead bodies and the wildlife has been severely damaged. Special services of purification were organized for the churches in which people had been massacred.

32. J. Wisdom, 'Tolerance', in *Paradox and Discovery*, Oxford 1965, 139–47.

33. Rutayisire, *Faith Under Fire* (n. 19), 108.

Asia: Sri Lanka

Vimal Tirimanna

Once upon a time, Sri Lanka was well-known for its natural beauty, tea, ancient Buddhist culture and hospitality. But today, the name Sri Lanka features prominently in the international mass media not so much for any of those, but mostly for terrorism and ethnic violence, as a result of the conflict between the Sri Lankan government and the Tamil militant organization, the Liberation Tigers of Tamil Eelam (LTTE), who are demanding a separate country in the north of Sri Lanka. In this article my intention is to examine rather skimpily how religion has contributed to the present situation of war and violence in Sri Lanka, with special reference to Buddhism.

Sri Lanka, formerly called 'Ceylon', is an island in the Indian Ocean, with a total area of 65,610 square kilometres. It is situated at the southern tip of the Indian sub-continent and is separated from the Indian mainland by 29 km. Today, the people who inhabit this island consist of diverse ethnic groups and religions. At the last official census in 1981, the ethnic composition of Sri Lanka's 14.8 million population was 73.98% Sinhalese, 12.60% Sri Lankan Tamils, 7.12% Moors, 5.56% Indian Tamils, 0.29% Malays, 0.26% Burghers and 0.20% others. The distribution of the adherents of the four major religions in the country were Buddhists 69.3%, Hindus 15.5%, Muslims 7.5% and Christians 7.6%.[1]

Historians believe that the Sinhalese were a people of Aryan origin who came to the island from Northern India, around 500 BC. They are of the opinion that the Sinhalese settlement and colonization of the island preceded the arrival of the Dravidian-Tamil settlers by several centuries.[2] Although Sri Lanka has almost always had Sinhalese rulers and kings ever since the Sinhalese colonized the island, as early as 237 BC, two Tamil kings from South India usurped the Sinhalese throne and ruled for twenty two years, and ten years later the South Indian Chola general Elara captured the Sinhalese capital Anuradhapura and ruled from there for forty-four years. With the rise of three powerful Dravidian-Hindu states in

South India in the fifth and sixth centuries, the Sinhalese kingdom in Sri Lanka experienced sporadic aggression. In the middle of the thirteenth century AD, the Tamils were able to establish their own kingdom in the Jaffna peninsula, in northern Sri Lanka, with the help of their South Indian brethren. This kingdom maintained its independent status till the beginning of the seventeenth century AD, except for a brief period in the middle of the fifteenth century AD when it came under the control of the Sinhalese ruler of the entire island.

Since Buddhism is the religion of the majority of the island and since it is the religion which really played a key role (either consciously or unconsciously, directly or indirectly) in arriving at the point of history where we are today, I shall discuss briefly the role played by Buddhism under the following headings. It is important to note here that I do not mean to say that *only* Buddhism played a role. Indeed, other religions, too, played their role. For example, Christianity, with its militant missionary approach in converting local Buddhists during the colonial period and with its dominance in the colonial educational system, also played a significant role, at least in being a major cause in the resurgence of Buddhist Sinhalese nationalism, as we shall see. But, within the limited space, I can consider only the role played by Buddhism.

I. The concepts of *sihadeepa* and *dhammadeepa*

According to the popular Sinhalese myth, the Sinhalese race descends from a *singha*, a lion. The story of Sinhabahu, their great ancestor, is part of the legendary history of the Sinhalese people. According to this story, Prince Sinhabahu and his twin sister were born in the country of Vangas in northern India, as a result of the union between a lion and a Vanga princess. Later, the union of the twins gave birth to Prince Vijaya, the traditional father of the Sinhalese race.[3] Prince Vijaya's ancestry and arrival in Sri Lanka are recorded dramatically in the great Sinhalese historical account written by the Buddhist monks, the *Mahavamsa*. Accordingly, the name given to the island is *sihadeepa*, which means 'the island of the Sinhalese, the descendants of the lion'.

According to another allied popular Sinhalese myth, at the very arrival in Sri Lanka of their ancestors led by Prince Vijaya, Lord Buddha passed into *nibbana*, and before he died, he summoned Sakka, the king of the gods, and made a special appeal to him to make Sir Lanka the place where his teachings would be cherished and guarded. The gods, at Buddha's request, enabled Prince Vijaya to conquer Sri Lanka. Moreover, popular mythical belief holds that the Buddha himself visited Sri Lanka three times, and thus hallowed three different places of the island, which are popular Buddhist pilgrim centres today. These visits are affirmed by the very first chapter of *Mahavamsa* itself. Accordingly, it was Buddha himself who was chiefly instrumental in expelling the original inhabitants of the island, the *yakkas* ('demons') and the *nagas* ('snakes'). Obeyesekere highlights the significance of this myth: 'the island has been consecrated by the Buddha himself, and evil forces have been banished or subjugated preparatory to the arrival of the founder of the Sinhalese race, Prince Vijaya'.[4] Thus, Sri Lanka is popularly conceived as the island of Buddhism, the island of *dhamma (dhammadeepa)*.

Moreover, Obeyesekere points out that from ancient times, there were two allied beliefs which reinforced the intimate link between the Sinhalese and Buddhism. 1. Not only was Sri Lanka consecrated by the Buddha himself but the Buddha was immanent in his relics enshrined in the great centres of Buddhist pilgrimage in Sri Lanka. 2. Two of these relics became associated with Sinhalese sovereignty and legitimacy of kingship.[5] Thus, popular belief holds that from the very beginning, both the Sinhalese race and Buddhist religion are closely associated. Accordingly, Sri Lanka is first and foremost the island of the Sinhalese Buddhists (*sihadeepa* and *dhammadeepa*). From this it flows that the island is the land of the Sinhalese and that it was destined to preserve the *dhamma* in its pristine purity with the help of the guardian deities and a king of the people, a Sinhalese king.

II. The concept of Sinhala Buddhist nationalism

As De Silva points out, Sri Lanka is the oldest Buddhist society in the world, and the country 'carries a huge burden of historical memories that have powerfully affected the link between religion, nationalism and politics in modern times'.[6] The historical experiences of sporadic conflicts with South Indian Dravidian invaders from the fifth century AD onwards created a new pattern of myth and mythicized history among the Sinhalese, which incorporated another theme: Sinhalese as defenders of the *sasana* (Buddhism) and Tamils who were Hindus, as opposers of the *sasana*. In the memory of the Sinhalese, the Tamils figured as the 'invaders' from South India. Undoubtedly, the epic description in *Mahawamsa* of the Sinhalese king Dutugemunu's triumph over Elara, the Tamil Chola general from South India who usurped the Sinhalese throne for forty-four years in the third century BC, reinforced such myths and memories. Time and again, Sinhalese people could be mobilized and activated by their rulers to fight foreign invaders by appealing to the sentiments underlying such myths and memories, so that these myths and memories became, on occasion, rallying points for Sinhalese nationalism.[7]

Needless to say, such appeals re-inforced the concept of *Sinhalese* Buddhism.

Until the advent of the European colonialists in the sixteenth century AD, in Sri Lanka being Buddhist implied being Sinhalese. Since then, as a result of the Christian missionary activities, some Sinhalese were converted to Christianity, at times even using Portuguese state machinery; thus, for the first time, being Sinhalese ceased to imply being Buddhist. Sinhalese ceased to be an ethnic identity, for henceforth there were Sinhalese Buddhists and Sinhalese Christians, the former considered by the masses as the true sons and daughters of the soil, while the latter were considered by them to be the 'accomplices' of the colonialists. Accordingly the real independence which the Lankans needed to gain was not merely independence from the European colonialists, but also independence from their 'accomplices' who were regarded as the heirs of the colonialists. To do this, it was necessary to stress not merely the independence of the Sri Lankans as such, but more precisely that of the Sinhalese *Buddhists*. It was in this sense that the eminent Sinhalese Buddhist revivalists like Anagarika Dharmapala and Harischandra Walisingha were clamouring for a place of primacy for Buddhism in the island. In the 1930s, there sprang up influential Sinhala/Buddhist revivalist movements like the Sinhala Maha Sabha, which urged a Sri Lankan polity which was essentially Buddhist *and* Sinhalese in orientation.

With the independence and the dawn of democratic native majority rule in 1948, the Buddhist Sinhalese cultural awakening which initially began as a protest against European colonialists underwent a populist twist. This twist received further impetus in the 1950s when majoritarian weight and democratic theory lent their support to Sinhalese Buddhist nationalism.[8] Sinhalese Buddhist nationalism received another great impetus in 1956, with the grand celebration of the *Buddha Jayanthi*, the 2500th anniversary of the death of the Buddha, which coincided with the 2500th anniversary of the founding of the Sinhalese race and the establishment of a settled government in the island. This event resulted in the publication of the book entitled *The Revolt in the Temple*, which according to many attempted to advance a Sinhalese Buddhist ideology.[9] With the election promise to make Sinhalese the only national language, S.W.R.D. Bandaranaika came to power with an overwhelming majority in the same year. Many regard this as another event that paved the way for the present ethnic conflict. All these events emphasized and exploited the intrinsic link between Buddhism and Sinhalese, which were so closely intertwined that it was impossible to treat either of them separately. De Silva comments on this very correctly: 'The crucial significance of the renewed link between language and religion was that Buddhist activism, which has been directed so far against the privileged position enjoyed by Christianity and Christians in Sri Lanka, shifted its attention to the Tamil minority as well.'[10]

The post-independence campaign for the supremacy of the Sinhalese Buddhists reached its climax with the promulgation of the Republican Constitution in 1972. This recognized Sinhalese as the national language and Buddhism as the state-protected religion, thus alienating minorities such as Tamils and Christians from the main stream of Sri Lankan politics. On the eve of the framing of the revised Constitution in 1978, the All Ceylon Buddhist Congress urged the government to make Buddhism 'the state religion', which implied that the main objectives of Buddhist revivalism were not yet achieved. The government turned down the request and repeated the 1972 Constitution with regard to the status of religions in Sri Lanka. One would agree that it was mainly this Sinhalese Buddhist nationalism which served as the immediate cause in the resurgence of the Sri Lankan Tamil nationalism that has culminated today in Sri Lankan Tamil separatism with its concept of *Eelam*, a separate Tamil country.

III. The role played by the *sangha*

One drastic change that took place after the arrival of the European colonialists in the island in the sixteenth century AD[11] was the loss of influence which the *sangha* (the Buddhist monks/Bhikkus) traditionally exerted in the running of the affairs of the country. From ancient times, the *sangha* played an extremely important role in the running of the state in Sri Lanka, especially in the form of giving counsel to the Sinhalese kings. Some writers even contend that ever since the arrival of Buddhism in Sri Lanka in the third century BC, the *sangha* had been an essential element in the governing of the country.[12] That is to say that there was a special link between the state and religion. The popular Sinhalese view has always been that it was the *sangha* which came to the rescue of the Sinhalese whenever the race was in peril. With the arrival of the European colonialists, the traditional ties of the *sangha* and the state were 'disestablished' for the first time in Sri Lanka.[13] Regaining this lost influence of the *sangha* over the state was high on the agenda of Sinhalese Buddhist nationalism even after independence. Surely this reinforced the Sinhalese *Buddhist* concept while alienating the Sinhalese Christians and the other minorities such as the Tamils, and added fuel to the ethnic conflict when the majority of the *sangha* insisted that only the Sinhalese Buddhists are the natives of the island. On the eve of the 1970 General Elections, a leading Buddhist monk scholar wrote an open letter to the then

Prime Minister, Dudley Senanayake, under the title, 'Is it an injustice to show special favour to Buddhism?', in which he argued that no injustice was done to the minorities by giving Buddhism primacy among the religions in the island.[14] There is no doubt that the effort made to recapture the lost importance of the *sangha* in the state ended up by consciously or unconsciously reinforcing the popular concept of Sinhalese Buddhist nationalism and, in the process, alienating minorities like Christians and Tamils.

This point is substantiated in a recent article written by an enlightened Buddhist monk (the type of which are very rare in Sri Lanka). 'In recent times the most severe problem our country has faced is the question of *Eelam*. Although we did not take the question very seriously until Tamil youth took up arms demanding a separate state, it now haunts the mind of every citizen. In this problem, too, the Buddhist Bhikkus have aligned themselves mainly on the basis of protecting the land of the Sinhala Buddhism from Eelamists. But unfortunately some of the statements and activities of our responsible Bhikkus whose perspective is "Sinhala Buddhism" have contributed not to the resolution of the problem but to aggravating it even further.'[15] Almost as if to substantiate this view further, on 20 October 1996, the Mahanayaka (Chief Buddhist Prelate) of Asgiriya referred to Sinhalese Buddhists as 'the natives of Sri Lanka', and went on to say: 'History records that it was the *sangha* that advised the rulers of the country how they should act to safeguard the motherland, the race and Buddhism. The present day leaders do not pay any heed to the representations made by the *sangha*. The country, race and Buddhism are in peril. The Sinhalese Buddhists of Sri Lanka are heading for the worst disaster that had ever befallen them because of the craving of the two principal political parties of the country to remain in power by pleasing the minority communities of the country.'[16]

IV. Colonial education system

From the time of the advent of the European colonialists, the Christian missionary organizations of various Christian denominations which accompanied them, such as the Roman Catholic Church, the Dutch Reformed Calvinist Churches and the Anglican Church, had viewed education as the principal vehicle of religious conversion. With the backing of the successive colonial powers, each denomination at one time or the other achieved a dominant position within the formal education structure of the country. Since most of the educated locals were mainly Christian or, if not, at least pro-missionary, and since they were the ones who dominated the echelons of power, the non-Christians, especially the Buddhists, perceived the need to counter this Christian upsurge and sought to create their own educational institutions which would provide an education within a Buddhist atmosphere; this would also enable them to recapture influential positions in the country, which were then mostly in the hands of Christian or pro-Christian groups. However, it should be noted that the majority of the pupils in the Christian missionary schools were not Christians, and that those with talent, whether Christian or non-Christian, were not debarred from social advancement, as numerous examples would testify.[17] The clamour that it is the majority Sinhalese Buddhists who ought to hold power and prestigious posts of Sri Lanka emerged as a part of Buddhist revivalism which in fact was a reaction against colonial Christian missionary activity, especially against the Christian grip on the country's education system. This Sinhalese Buddhist clamour achieved its main goal when almost all the Christian schools were nationalized in the early 1960s. But this popular clamour did not stop there; it completed its victory when in the early 1970s the government introduced a standardized system based on the geographical districts with regard to the admissions to the limited seats in the local universities. This system, with its own merits and demerits, formally shut the door on many Tamil students from Northern Tamil districts who had better aggregates in their exmaination marks. Students with less aggregates from schools in rural areas with less facilities in undeveloped districts (most of whom turned out to be Sinhalese) were given preference in local university admissions. The Tamils perceived this move as a discriminaton against them; this was a major cause for the frustration of the Tamil youth militants who took up arms, demanding *Eelam*.

Conclusion

In the above discussion, I have endeavoured to demonstrate how religion has played a role in the ethnic conflict of Sri Lanka, taking Buddhism as a model. At least in the context of Sri Lanka, discriminatory myths and popular beliefs which are based on religion have contributed largely to the present situation of war and violence. It is in this sense that I have tried to demonstrate the conscious or the unconscious role played by Buddhism – to be precise, fanatic Sinhalese Buddhism – in instigating the Sinhalese-Tamil conflict and the outbreak of violence.

Notes

1. *Statistical Handbook of the Democratic Socialist Republic of Sri Lanka*, Colombo 1984, 13.

2. K. M. de Silva, 'Historical Survey', in K. M. de Silva (ed.), *Sri Lanka: A Survey*, London 1977, 32–7.

3. For further details of this myth see R. Weerakoon, *Sri Lanka's Mythology*, Colombo 1985, 118–35.

4. Gannanath Obeyesekere, 'The Vicissitudes of the Sinhala-Buddhist Identity through Time and Change', in Michael Roberts (ed.), *Collective Identities. Nationalisms and Protest in Modern Sri Lanka*, Colombo 1979, 281.

5. Ibid., 286–7.

6. K. M. de Silva, 'Buddhist Revivalism, Nationalism and Politics in Modern Sri Lanka', in James Warner Byorkman (ed.), *Fundamentalism, Revivalists and Violence in South Asia*, Riverdale, Maryland 1988, 109.

7. Obeyesekere, 'Vicissitudes' (n. 4), 283.

8. Michael Roberts, 'Meanderings in the Pathways of Collective Identity and Nationalism', in id. (ed.), *Collective Identities* (n. 4), 7.

9. W. A. Wiswa Warnapala, *The Sri Lankan Political Scene*, New Delhi 1993, 222.

10. De Silva, 'Buddhist Revivalism' (n. 6), 136.

11. Sri Lanka had three European colonial powers: the Portuguese (1505–1658), the Dutch (1658–1796) and the British (1796–1948).

12. Ven. Havanpola Ratanasana, 'Calling for a Positive Role for Bhikkus in the National Leadership', in *Religion and Development in Asian Societies*, Colombo 1974, 18.

13. Heinz Bechert, 'Buddhism as a Factor of Political Modernization: The Case of Sri Lanka', in ibid., 10–11.

14. Ratanasana, 'Calling for a Positive Role for Bhikkus' (n. 12), 24.

15. Ven. Uttarananda Thera. 'Sinhala Buddhist Monks and the Rights of the Tamils', *Dialogue*, New Series XVIII, Nos. 1–3, January-December 1991, 6.

16. As reported in *The Island*, 22 October 1996, 1.

17. Michael Roberts, 'Elite Formation and Elites. 1832–1931', in Roberts (ed.), *Collective Identities* (n. 4), 189.

Europe: Bosnia

Miroslav Volf

A perfect hell on earth

'There are no devils left in hell,' the missionary said, 'they are all in Rwanda.' Rwanda – people being hunted down on the streets like animals and killed where they were caught; blood flowing down the aisles of the churches which, by a perverse inversion of symbolism, were made into preferred places of massacre; butchered bodies floating down the river on their way to Ethiopia, via the short cut of the Nayaborongo river, from where the hated Tutsi 'intruders' came. 'Fighting was hand to hand,' writes a reporter, 'intimate and unspeakable, a kind of bloodlust that left those who managed to escape it hollow-eyed and mute.'[1] In only three months a million were left dead and more than twice as many were driven out of their homes.

'There are no devils left in hell, they are all in Rwanda.' The words seem to paint just the right image to express the unfathomable. Yet if we leave the immediacy of Rwandan brutalities and consider the larger world, we sense that the image is skewed on two important counts. First, not *all* devils are in Rwanda. If the missionary's words were not a cry of desperation, one might even be able to detect in them a tinge of clandestine racism: a little country in black Africa has sucked up all the black devils. What about Bosnia? What about Nagorno-Karabakh? What about all the fifty spots around the globe – Western countries included – where violence has taken root between people who share the same terrain but differ in ethnicity, race, language or religion? No devils there? Without wanting to diminish the horror of Rwanda's genocide, all the devils of vicious ethnic strife are by no means there. They are dispersed around the globe, sowing death and desolation, even if less vehemently than the devils of Rwanda.

The second way in which the missionary's comment on Rwanda is skewed is even more disturbing than the first. The global spread of the devils notwithstanding, hell is by no means an empty place. In the dark kingdom of evil potencies new armies are being trained for fresh assignments. Rapid population growth, diminishing resources, un-employment, migration to shanty cities and lack of education are steadily increasing pressure along the many social fault-lines of our globe. Though we cannot predict exactly when and where social quakes will occur and how powerful they will be, we can be sure that the earth will shake.[2]

As the image of 'fault-lines' suggests, clashes will take place along the boundary lines of social groups. Today, after the breakdown of a bipolar world, social tectonic plates are defined less by ideology than by culture. As Samuel Huntington argues, on the global scale the fault-lines between major civilizations – the broadest level of cultural identity people have – 'will be the battle lines of the future'.[3] Similarly, within civilizations and on their borders, the coming wars will be fought between discrete cultural and ethnic groups. Conditions seem ripe for more Rwandas and Bosnias in the future. The kingdom of darkness has not exhausted its resources. There are more devils in hell ready to make more hells on earth.

Rwandas and Bosnias of today and tomorrow challenge the churches to rethink their mission as agents of peace. What vision of the relations between cultures do we have to offer to communities at war?

Exclusion and embrace[4]

To see the issue of ethnic conflict in the right perspective we need adequate categorial lenses. Under the influence of liberation theologies, in recent decades the categories of 'oppression' and 'liberation' have ruled theological reflection on social issues. They were designed to handle experiences of economic exploitation and political domination, and they did that job reasonably well.

However, the categories are inadequate, even detrimental, in dealing with cultural conflicts. The trouble is that, in a sense, they fit conflict-situations too well: *both* Hutus and Tutsis, *both* Croats and Serbs, see themselves as oppressed and engaged in the struggle for liberation. The categories of 'oppression' and 'liberation' provide each with moral weapons that make their battles so much deadlier. Moreover, in many situations of ethnic conflict we do not have a clear perpetrator and a clear victim; both parties have oppressed and both have suffered oppression, though often in varying degrees and at different junctures in their common history. Even when the perpetrator can clearly be named – as in the case of Nazi Germany or apartheid South Africa – we need much more than simply to liberate the oppressed by defeating the oppressor. Since the former oppressors and the oppressed must continue living together as neighbours, we must work towards reconciliation. 'Liberation' does this only to a limited extent.

To help resolve conflicts between peoples we need a different set of categories. These must both name the evil committed by one or both parties and facilitate reconciliation between them. I suggest that the categories of 'exclusion' and 'embrace' do precisely that. These are the central categories of what I have called 'a theology of embrace'. A theology of embrace is not meant to replace theologies of liberation, but to relocate these theologies by inserting them into a larger theological framework which will both preserve their strengths and curtail their weaknesses. It is from the perspective of a theology of embrace that I approach the problem of ethnic strife here.

When ethnic groups lock horns, they become obsessed with purity. Blood must be pure: German blood alone should run through German veins, free from all non-Aryan contamination. Territory should be pure: Serbian soil must belong to Serbs, cleansed of all non-Serbian intruders. We want our world to ourselves and so we create a monochrome world without 'others'; we want to be identical with ourselvs, so we exclude 'others'. As Nicholas Wolterstorff observes, when an ideology of ethnic purity kicks in, the 'others' who happen to reside among us are left with 'only two choices: either to emigrate, under varying degrees of duress, or to accept the status of second-class citizens, with varying degrees of deprivation of rights and repression. There is never any other choice.'[5]

Before excluding others from one's social world, however, one must drive them out, as it were, from one's symbolic world. Commenting in *The Conquest of America* on the Spaniards' genocide of the native Americans, Tzvetan Todorov writes:

> The desire for wealth and the impulse to master – certainly these two forms of aspiration to power motivate the Spaniards' conduct; but this conduct is also conditioned by their notion of the Indians as inferior beings, halfway between men and beasts. Without this essential premise, the destruction could not have taken place.[6]

With somewhat more nuance than on the shores of the New World in the sixteenth century, the pattern of debasement is being repeated today in many parts of the world: the 'others' are first dehumanized or demonized and then discriminated against, driven out or destroyed. Even in the Western capitalist societies, where explicit and public exclusion is forbidden by formal rules, implicit and private exclusion still takes place, often in the form of unconscious but nonetheless effectual aversion.

There are many reasons why 'others' are excluded, driven out of our world. To start with the most innocent, we strive to get rid of that which blurs accepted boundaries, disturbs our social identity and disarranges our symbolic cultural maps. Often, however, dehumanization and consequent destruction of 'others' are a projection of our own individual or collective hatred of ourselves. 'Others' become scapegoats, concocted from our own shadows as repositories of our sins so we can relish the illusion of our sinless superiority.

Both of these accounts of exclusion are important because they help us understand why Jews could be killed just because they were Jews or Blacks lynched just because they were Blacks. Yet neither account of exclusion will suffice. We do not exclude others simply because we like the way things are or hate the way we are, but because we desire what others have. Ronald Takaki points out in *A Different Mirror*, for instance, that barbarization and demonization of the indigenous population in North America 'occurred within the economic context of competition over land'.[7]

In the Bible both symbolic and practical exclusion are named as sin. The prophet Isaiah announces judgment against those who dispossess and drive out others so that they alone can be the masters of the land (5. 8f).

- Ah, you who join house to house,
        who add field to field,
    until there is room for no one but you,
        and you are left alone in the midst of the land.
    The Lord of hosts has sworn in my hearing,
        'Surely many houses shall be desolate,
    large and beautiful houses, without inhabitants.'

Those who have driven others out will themselves be driven out of the clean world they have created for themselves.

Consider the birth of Gentile mission in the Acts of the Apostles as an account of how symbolic exclusion is named as sin and overcome. The apostles were unwilling to have the gospel cross the boundaries of an ethnic group and become the good news for all tribes and nations. Before they can venture on a Gentile mission the inherited notions of purity and uncleanness must be dismantled. 'What God has made clean,' the voice said to Peter in a vision, 'you must not call profane' (Acts 10.15). Falsely to call things profane and to purge them, to exclude others through prejudice or violence, is sin, and it must be unmasked and exposed. For all human beings are all equally worthy of respect because they are created in the image of God.

However, we may not allow the critique of exclusion to deteriorate into a polemic against all boundaries that order social space, a tendency in the circles influenced by postmodern thought. As Manfred Franke points out in a critique of the postmodernist Michael Foucault:

It is impossible (and unappealing even for pure fantasy) to fight against all order and advocate a pure, abstract non-order. For, much like the mythical tohuwabohu, a non-order would be a 'creature' with no attributes, a place where one could distinguish nothing and where neither happiness nor pleasure, neither freedom nor justice, could be identified.[8]

Boundaries must remain, because without boundaries you have non-order, and non-order is not the end of oppression but the end of life. What must be abolished are the false boundaries which pervert an order that sustains and nourishes human life, shaping it into a system of exclusions that degrades and destroys it. The warped system of exclusions – what people 'call profane' – must be dismantled in the name of an order of things which God, the creator and sustainer of life, 'has made clean'. In contrast to the 'system of exclusion', which rests on prejudice and oppression, I will call this divine order that sustains life in its rich diversity 'an order of embrace'.

But what is an 'embrace'? Let me try to answer this question by looking first at the ambivalence of group identities. Around the globe today we are experiencing a resurgence of what has been called 'new tribalism' – reaffirmation of group identities. On the one hand, this is a salutory process. There is a growing realization that the Enlightenment ideal of abstract humanity is truncated; we encounter people not simply as 'humans', stripped of their culture, skin, colour or gender, but as Hutus or Tutsi, as Buddhist or Hindu, as red or yellow, as men or women. Group identities offer us homes to belong in, spaces where we can be among our own and therefore ourselves. They also provide us with bases of power from which we can pursue our goals or engage in the struggle against oppression.

However, in addition to being salutary, the resurgence of group identities is deeply troubling. The homes which group identities provide can be stifling, suppressing the difference and creativity of their non-conformist members. Bases of power can become fortresses into which we retreat, surrounding ourselves by impenetrable walls dividing 'us' from 'them'. In situations of conflict, they serve as encampments from which to undertake raids into the enemy territory. Group identities are profoundly ambivalent: they are havens of belonging as well as repositories of aggression; suffocating enclosures as well as bases of liberating power.

Notice the location at which the blessing of group identities slips into a curse. It is the desire for purity, for homogeneity, for a monochrome world without the other. Non-conformist members must be repressed, outsiders must be kept at bay, even destroyed. What compounds the trouble is that pure communal identities are so many pure illusions. They are but dark dreams of people unwilling or unable to face the colourful social realities. As Edward Said points out, 'all culture is hybrid . . . and encumbered, or entangled with what used to be regarded as extraneous elements'.[9] There are always strangers within our gates, and we ourselves never belong completely to a given group but only in part. We live in overlapping social territories, belong to overlapping traditions. Our communities are like our domicile in which we feel at home, yet keep rearranging, taking old things out and bringing new things in, often objects acquired on visits to near and distant places, objects which symbolize that we can never be the same after we have ventured out of our home, that things we encounter 'outside' become a part of the 'inside'.

This brings me to the metaphor of 'embrace'. In an embrace I open my arms to create space in myself for the other. Open arms are a sign that I do not want to be by myself only. They are an invitation for the other to come in and feel at home with me. In an embrace I also close my arms around the other. Closed arms are a sign that I want the other to become a part of me while at the same time I maintain my own identity. By becoming part of me, the other enriches me. In a mutual embrace, neither has remained the same because both have been enriched by each other, and yet both have remained true to their genuine selves.

Embrace, I believe, is what takes place between the three persons of the holy Trinity, which is a divine model of human community. The Johannine Jesus says: 'The Father is in me and I am in the Father' (John 10. 38). The one divine person is not that person only, but includes the other divine persons in itself: it is what it is only through the indwelling of the other. The Son is the Son because the Father and the Spirit indwell him; without this interiority of the Father and the Spirit, there would be no Son. Every divine person *is* the other persons, but he is the other persons in his own particular way.

Embrace, I propose, is what should happen between different ethnic or cultural groups. Instead of seeking to isolate ourselves from other groups by insisting on our pure identity, we should open ourselves to one another to be enriched by our differences. Of course, we will have to maintain group boundaries. If we did not, the bright colours of cultural multi-formity would wash out into a drab grey of cultural sameness. We must cultivate our languages, sustain our traditions, nurture our cultures. And all this requires boundary maintenace. At the same time, boundaries must be porous. Guests should be welcomed and we should pay visits to our near and distant neighbours so that through cross-fertilization our respective cultures thrive, correcting and enriching each other.

However, though crucial, cultural exchange is not yet cultural embrace. As Peter L. Berger notes in *A Far Glory*:

It is one of the more facetious illusions of liberal ideology that people will like each other better by getting to know each other. The opposite is the case, as a glance at the homicide data will show. Most murders are committed by close friends and relatives.[10]

Berger goes on to say that 'the adage that good fences make good neighbours has certain sociological validity' (p.38). Yet even if knowledge and porous borders do not suffice, the solution to our communal feuds certainly does lie in better fences and deeper ignorance. Rather, in addition to knowledge of the other we need the *will* to welcome the other into our world.

Sometimes, as we all know, the others are not simply pleasant guests, but evil enemies. And even when they do us no harm, they seem strange, unknown, like some 'dark angels that muddle the transparency' of our world.[11] How do we embrace them? The answer is complicated and I can do no more here than to refer to my *Exclusion and Embrace*,[12] where I explore the issue at length. But this much can and must be said: a seed of embrace needs to be planted in our hearts by the spirit of embrace. We must be gripped by a vision of a new world in which all peoples retain their identity and yet are enriched in communion with other peoples, in which all will speak their own languages and yet be understood, and in which all will have their needs met because over their borders bridges will be built, venues of mutual giving and receiving (see Acts 2).

Notes

1. Nancy Gibbs, 'Why? The Killing Fields of Rwanda', *Time*, 16 May 1994, 57–63.
2. See Paul Kennedy, *Preparing for the Twenty-First Century*, New York and London 1994.
3. Samuel P. Huntington, 'The Clash of Civilizations?', *Foreign Affairs* 72, 1993, 22–49: 22.
4. For a fuller discussion of the following see my *Exclusion and Embrace. A Theological Exploration of Identity, Otherness and Reconciliation*, Nashville 1996.
5. Nicholas Wolterstorff, *Until Justice and Peace Embrace*, Grand Rapids 1983, 114.
6. Tzvetan Todorov, *The Conquest of America: The Question of the Other*, New York 1984, 146.
7. Ronald Takaki, *A Different Mirror: A History of Multicultural America*, Boston 1993.
8. Manfred Frank, *Was ist Neostrukturalismus?*, Frankfurt 1984.
9. Edward W. Said, *Culture and Imperialism*, New York 1993, 317.
10. Peter L. Berger, *A Far Glory: The Quest for Faith in an Age of Credulity*, New York 1992, 38.
11. Julia Kristeva, *Fremde sind wir uns selbst*, Frankfurt 1990, 11.
12. See note 4.

Latin America: Guatemala/ El Salvador

Jon Sobrino

A. Outbreak

Religion can – and does – generate fundamentalism, fanaticism, aggression, holy wars, and suicidal acts of martyrdom. This is the general premise of this issue of *Concilium*, in which the guiding question is 'Is religion a source of violence?' and in which for this section articles are grouped under the general heading of 'Religion and Violence; Outbreak and Overcoming'.

Speaking of the violence unleashed in Central America in the form of repression, wars and revolutions, we need to make one thing clear at the outset: in these countries, it is not religion that has been at the origin of violence, but injustice, the fruit of capitalism. Religion has therefore found itself caught up in a violence it has not generated. Religious reactions to this violence have varied, but the most noteworthy and specific has been that put forward by liberation theology: in the first place, to promote the struggle against violence; in the second, to bring out the redemption of violence, once this has been unleashed in the form of war and repression. This is what I set out to analyse here.

I. Analogy of violence

In Central America – Nicaragua, Guatemala and El Salvador – there has been no cult of violence in the name of religion, but there has been in the name of injustice – institutionalized injustice, as Medellin called it. And one has to say that in this Medellin has not been surpassed, though it is widely ignored today.

(a) The analogatum princeps *of violence: structural injustice*

Terrorism, massacres and wars are the cruellest and most repellent expression of violence, but they are not the true source of violence, nor the most productive of violence or its most permanent form. This has to be sought in what Medellin called structural injustice, which 'conspires against peace' (*Peace*, 1) and is in itself 'institutionalized violence' (*Peace*, 16).

Injustice is violence in the strict sense because it deprives majorities – unjustly and by force – of the basics of life and of life itself. It is the most real violence, quantitatively by its massive scale, qualitatively by its spread. The poor are in effect those who live 'bent' (*anaw*) under the weight of existence so that their main task is simply to survive; they are the in-significant, those who have no dignity or worth (*ne-pios*, meaning both poor and wordless); they are the im-potent, those who have no power to claim their rights; they are, more and more, the in-existent, those who do not exist for the productive economic apparatus.

This injustice is, at least in these countries, the root of all other violences, although in Guatemala ethnic roots also have to be taken into account. It is also the easiest to hide, since its images do not strike with the force of the Holocaust or Hiroshima. And in the end it is the most difficult to eradicate, since its roots are the deepest and it does not usually produce the minimum of uneasy conscience necessary for conversion. Holocausts and massacres have produced Nuremberg trials, but the depradations of the continent of Latin America and the exploitaton of the continent of Africa have not. Faced with the barbarity of the Great Lakes, what tribunal has brought the Western powers to account for what happened in the last century?

Dives and Lazarus are even farther apart, and the Western world has not reacted as it should in the face of this gigantic primary 'institutionalized violence'. James Gustave Speth, administrator of the UN development programme, says that in poverty we are moving 'from the unjust to the inhuman'.[1] And this violence is also the most lasting, since even after wars have ended, poverty still rules and deals death. Nicaragua is now poorer than ever, seventeen years after the end of the revolutionary war. In El Salvador, as Bishop Orlando Cabrera has said, 'we are worse off than during the war. . . .Poverty, in our day, is denounced by itself since we live with it.'

(b) Accompanying violence: repression, war, state terrorism

The original violence is also the source of violence. Economic authorities defend injustice with the aid of the military and of 'death squads', who have committed veritable atrocities. And let us not forget, when we talk of 'wars in Central America', that before (and during) the wars there was 'repression', without having to subsume this into the more civilized and accepted concept of 'war', since state repression is not so much war-like as holocaust-like.

Those who carry out this accompanying violence (repression and war) are not – again – religious fanatics, but organizations and authorities accepted by the West, even sometimes put forward as models for Third World countries: governments and local oligarchies, encouraged and supported, in the case of Central America, by the government of the United States, its army, the CIA, the FBI, and tolerated in practice by Congress.[2] This fact is essential in order to grasp the root of violence in our world – which so far has nothing to do with religion.

(c) Revolutionary response violence

Against these two forms of violence, revolutionary violence broke out in Nicaragua, Guatemala and El Salvador, with the following characteristics. It was, above all, a violence made inevitable by the intolerable oppression and repression; it was a violence in self-defence or, more precisely, in defence of an oppressed people; its objective was to change radically a situation of injustice; its means were basically warlike and largely guided by ethical dictates.

This violence was judged legitimate by the bishops of Nicaragua after the Sandinista Revolution broke out; Archbishop Romero also affirmed its possible legitimacy in El Salvador, though he did everything possible to prevent it from breaking out there. In many cases, the revolutionary fighters gave proof of great love for the people, but that said, this violence also produced extreme physical evils, in lost lives and destruction; it succumbed to terrorism and the sinfulness inherent in the human condition, and its initial idealism – with some exceptions – often degenerated into pragmatism, protagonism, purges and corruption. (I deal with these negative by-products in the second half of this article.)

(d) Lessons not to be forgotten

The above used to be well known, but is now generally overlooked. Yet it is important to come back to it, because it teaches several important lessons.

The first is that our world is thoroughly violent, and it is vital to discover which of the many roots of this violence is the basic one. In Central America, this has been and still is capitalism (under any of its many faces) and not religion. More generally, we can ask whether, in this century, 'the cruellest known to history' (Hannah Arendt), religion was at the basis of the two world wars and the more than one hundred other smaller ones that have followed; if it was the prime cause of the great symbols of barbarity in this century – Auschwitz, Hiroshima, the Gulags, and more recent ones such as Rwanda and Haiti.

The second is that in this part of the world, capitalism produces two kinds of violence, so that we can speak of the analogy of violence. Seen from the cruelty and repression it causes, the *analogatum princeps* of violence is repression, massacres, the Holocaust. Seen from its extent and duration, the *analogatum princeps* is the injustice that produces poverty and slow death. Capitalism is responsible for both these.

The third lesson is the need for memory, since what I have just described is generally covered over and forgotten, specifically the violence produced by capitalism. Hence the need for memory, a theological category of the first order in both the Old and New Testaments, as J. B. Metz has recently emphasized, speaking of the *memoria passionis*. Elie Wiesel wrote these self-evident words of Auschwitz: 'People resist remembering. They cannot live with the truth and think they can live against truth. But although we are few and will become steadily fewer, we must go on remembering.' And just as we should remember Auschwitz, so we must remember the inhumanity of Central American capitalism. Otherwise, we are dragged into a culture of unreality, as though in reality 'these things do not happen', and impunity is added to forgetfulness with the greatest of ease.[3]

The fourth lesson is where to place religion in the whole queston of violence. It is not enough to examine whether religion generates violence through its fundamentalism, which is not the case in Central America, though it is in other parts of the world; we must also examine whether religion is justifying or facilitating any form of violence, particularly that generated by capitalism, as happens in the United States. In other words, we need to ask if religion is reinforcing economic and political fundamentalism, which has the violent dynamism of any fundamentalism.

Finally, a reflection on the way religion can possibly be blackmailed today. In the world we live in, it is seen as bad taste and contrary to the aesthetics of current geopolitics to recall the conflictivity of the actual situation, so we are put on our guard – and rightly – against the potential of religions for aggressivity. It is true that – at least for a time – tragedies such as that of Rwanda cannot be hushed up, but the twenty or thirty million human beings who die of hunger every year are calmly ignored. Political and economic discourse tends to gloss over things like that, while exalting the benefits of the global economy and the world market and propounding the right paths of dialogue and tolerance. Now in this world, religious discourse sounds 'out of tune'; it 'grates'. This is because religion, or at least Christianity, is orientated toward peace, certainly, but is also 'the guardian of prophecy and of the memory of sin', and to take both things seriously means both unmasking conflicts and, in a sense, provoking them. Religion should not of course originate violence, but neither can it be silent about the truth of the present situation – even if this leads to some type of conflict.

II. Manipulated religion and liberating religion

Injustice, not religion, lies at the root of violence in Central America, but once this violence has been unleashed, religion has played a variety of roles.

(a) Religion used and manipulated in the service of injustice

Structural injustice has no religious motivation, but it has in the past sought support in traditional religious values and is now doing so in the sects.

In relation to traditional religious values, the phenomenon is well known: even the most barbaric systems look for a religious justification, as though they were combatting irreligion (atheism, communism) or defending divine values (property, worship, religion itself). In reality, primary violence (injustice, neo-liberalism, the market) is not in the least concerned with religious values, but it is interested in the support it can derive from these. So in this case the most basic fundamentalism should not be sought in the religious sphere, but in the economic, which does unleash total violence, as we saw clearly in the years of 'national security' regimes. And so countries as little religious as those can just as well originate or sustain violence as those of Central America. They have a 'fundamentalism' distinct from the religious kind, but which coincides with it on one essential point: the decision never to question the *status quo*, which is regarded as something absolutely ultimate (divine). And not even atrocities such as those of Rwanda can make this 'fundamentalism' of capital waver.

Religion, then, is used to justify the violence that derives from the defence of capitalism, even though this extends to repression, terrorism and war, by presenting capitalism as the defender of religion and the enemy of irreligion. In Central America this has happened with the support of certain bishops, even if they have not gone to the extremes reached by some Argentinian bishops during the military dictatorship there.

Where sects are concerned, these have been upheld as the antidote to the – new – phenomenon of religion as a liberating force. As it would be hopeless to try to deprive entire peoples of their religious values and their liberating potential – something the West would do with a clear conscience if necessary, not to introduce these peoples to the benefits of 'enlightenment', but to remove a possible obstacle to its age-old expansionism – other ways have been tried. One – the crudest – has been persecution, something that has to be borne very much in mind in speaking of violence and religion, since in Central America, rather than generate violence, religion has suffered it 'in its flesh'. Another way has been to lend religious dignity to the system by working out a theology of capitalism, which, without blinking an eyelid, relates the kingdom of God to the market, as senior officials of the International Monetary Fund have done, and the Servant of Yahweh to the business community, as Michael Novak has done. But there is another way that has proved more widespread and effective, which is using evangelical sects.

These sects deserve respect, since they seek to offer solutions to basic human problems – marginalization, indignity, orphanage, and the like – which the historical churches have not adequately resolved, but they practise an alienating religion and are manipulated by injustice. The basic alienation consists in their elevating a-politicism to a religious ideal, which results in their failing to offer any resistance to injustice and the violence that goes with it. In El Salvador, governments have allowed, and even encouraged, the proliferation of these sects and their widespread activities.

(b) 'Liberating' religion: the struggle against injustice

Together with these forms of religious expression in Central America, a liberating set of religious, pastoral and theological values has emerged, which has been made responsible for encouraging Christians to engage in the sort of revolutionary struggle that is inspired by Marxism and results in Leninism. In the second part of this article I look more closely at what is most specific and Christian in liberation theology on the subject of violence – struggling against injustice and redeeming violence – but here I want to examine whether and how it relates to the violence capitalism has unleashed in Central America.

It is true that liberation theology has defended the possibility of Christian participation in an armed struggle under the traditional conditions – in which there is nothing new – and has also regarded it as natural that Christians should struggle against injustice together with Marxist revolutionaries. It is also true that the revolutionary Left has, from whatever motives, looked to this liberating religion as an ally in its struggle.

This is true, to varying degrees in each case, but it does not indicate the deepest aspect of the relationship between violence and liberating religion. This is anti-violent, since it is absolutely against the causes of violence, but through faithfulness to biblical revelation and historical reality it insists on the conflictive dimension of reality and the agonistic (struggling) dimension of human beings, which means they must take flesh in this conflictive reality and struggle within it against evil.

Liberation theology, in effect, insists on the exclusive and oppositional structure of reality. So its christology makes the kingdom of God central – which other christologies find it difficult to do – but *against* the anti-kingdom. It analyses the resurrection from the saving action of God, but *against* the crucifying action of the executioners. It analyses grace, but *against* sin. In a word, liberation theology takes absolutely seriously the dimension of negativity with which reality is shot through and which we have to face up to.

Summarily expressed, this theology presupposes a historical and theological structure of reality, which can be described in the following terms. The God of life *and* the idols of death co-exist in history. There also co-exist mediations of the will of God corresponding to these divinities: the kingdom of God *and* the anti-kingdom (societies that lead to death: the *pax Romana*, and a group based around the Temple, in Jesus' time). Mediators also co-exist: Jesus on the one hand, *and* the high priests, Pilate and his like, on the other. Now these two series of realities exist in a way that is mutually exclusive and also oppositional; that is, they are *by their nature* at odds with one another. The *and* therefore, by its nature, becomes *against*.

To give this its most intense expression: faith in the true God comes about simultaneously against the cult of idols, divinities of death. The other gods are not only inane, but, as the first commandment states, they are 'before me'. They are this for Jesus also: 'You cannot serve two masters'. The question of God – that is, the question of ultimate reality – is posed dialectically from the existence of various gods between whom we have to choose, and – in clarifying the inexorability of having to choose – Jesus makes the conflictivity of the choice clear: serving one means hating the other. For Jesus, the question to us human beings is not only if we believe in God, but also which god we do not believe in 'and' which god we 'hate'.

This is the nub of the question posed by the theme of violence for liberation theology. This theology has not – obviously – created the conflictivity of history, but it gives voice to it, and as something basic, in such a way that remaining silent about this conflictivity is an act – and a basic one – of dishonesty and connivance with the violence that gives rise to injustice. It might be said that this is dangerous and that it would be better to examine the concert of religions and philosophies for more conciliatory visions of reality, in which opposites complement one another. Whatever one thinks of this choice in theory, it is clear that, pastorally, it has to be presented in such a way it cannot, even unwittingly, propitiate a mystique of violence. But, having said that, it remains true that in the reading liberation theology makes of revelation and history, conflictivity is inherent in them,[4] and that one has to situate oneself within it in the best way possible.

Today there is little or no talk of conflictivity and antagonism as essential to history: we prefer more all-embracing idologies. In this way we try – from within our cultural ideology and environment – to minimize violence and diminish human aggressivity. Liberation theology, for its part, also seeks the end of violence, but it is not pacifist in the last resort. It does not hide the reality of conflict, even knowing that this will not facilitate, at least initially, solving the problem of violence. But incarnation, yesterday as well as today, necessarily takes place in a conflictive setting. The practice of mercy and the option for the poor have an intrinsic element of acting against the executioners – in the most human way possible. Christian anthropology is agonistic, struggling, because sin must be eradicated, not just forgiven.

In this sense, what has happened in Central America is very novel: the Christian faith, in the reading made of it by liberation theology, has led to a struggle – which has to be described with great precision. In the first place, it is a struggle of response, in defence of others, not in defence of religion itself. In the second place, it is a struggle against injustice and oppression, like the struggle of God and Jesus against oppressors and for the oppressed. In the third place, it is a struggle that takes place on different levels and using different instruments: word, organization, holiness.[5] Finally, Christians can choose, following their conscience, to take part in armed struggle, if the necessary ethical conditions are in place.

All this means that liberating religious feeling is honest with reality. Out of honesty it sets itself within a reality that is conflictive, struggles against the originating violence, and admits the possibility of an armed struggle in response. And out of the same honesty it warns against the negative by-products of all violence, even that which is legitimate and necessary. And however difficult it may be to hold to all these attitudes at once, it prefers to maintain the tension rather than solve the problem simplistically. This is what I propose to go on to analyse.

B. Overcoming

I said earlier that in Central America violence broke out independently of religion. For Christians with a liberating religious view the problem consisted in allowing themselves to be affected to a proper degree by the historical reality and the magnitude of the tragedy, and in responding to these in a Christian fashion – that is, by developing a 'spirituality in time of violence'. This means shedding light on violence, humanizing it and redeeming it. This seems to me to be the most specific contribution of liberation theology.

I. Shedding light on violence: the struggle against the ideal of wealth

I have already alluded to this, but now I want to tackle it directly. Accompanying violence and violence in response depend substantially on the original source of violence. This means that overcoming violence is above all overcoming the antecedent injustice that gives rise to violence, and if this does not happen, it is useless, empty and hypocritical to lament and criticize the violence that follows. This overcoming supposes struggling against the original source of violence, so that without this agonistic dimension of faith we are tolerating injustice and propitiating violence. This struggle does not have to be armed or military, and of course it cannot be terrorist, but it has to be a struggle – ideological, prophetic, utopian, critical, constructive, though in the end a struggle against the original source of violence.

Liberation theology has made this eradication of injustice a key point, and that is why Ignacio Ellacuria said that it is the most anti-violent of all theologies. I am not going to labour this point here, except to say that this seems to be its most novel and decisive contribution: to have elevated the struggle against injustice to a theological, not just an ethical, level. In other words, injustice is not merely a moral evil, but a theological reality: it is an idol. Shedding light on idols is the first thing liberation theology has – logically – done in its struggle against violence. Let us examine this.

Juan Luis Segundo, shortly after Medellín (1968), expressed the suspicion that theology was covering over the problem of idolatry, and that the Western world was the victim of a monumental deceit in making idolatry a thing of the past – a deceit it also strove to maintain at all costs. Therefore, his 1970 book on God begins with this shocking statement: 'My reflection begins by concerning itself much more with the – apparently out of fashion – antithesis faith-idolatry than with the – apparently current – faith-atheism.'[6] And his reason for beginning in this way is that, in our way of relating to the divine reality, 'we human beings proceed in order of importance like this: first, acting rightly in history; second, conceiving of God in terms of light or darkness; third, declaring whether God exists or not.'[7]

What is fundamental in this approach is its making praxis central (that it should be 'right') and its posing the theological problem in specifically dialectical form: not only whether something ultimate exists or not, but whether ultimate realities exist that are in mutually exclusive and antagonistic relationship. Stressing this is of the greatest importance, since modern theology has uncritically accepted that its pole of reference (expressed from the negative) is atheism (the non-existence of God) and not idolatry (the existence of gods), so that the latter remains hidden and can continue to act without feeling threatened. J. L. Sicre recognized that this is the case in his 1979 *Los dioses olvidados*, 'The Forgotten Gods' ('hidden' would be my preferred term). In this introduction, he says that idolatry seems to have become a museum piece, with no live interest or currency for most scripture scholars.

The reason for this forgetting may lie in the ingenuous – or self-interested, rather – assumption that idolatry is expressed essentially on a religious and cultural level and is therefore not a problem for enlightened Western societies. So Sicre shows that idolatry is almost always studied under two aspects – the use of images in the Yahwist cult and the cult of pagan gods. This is a strictly cultic viewpoint, concentrating on concerns many centuries old, but not on those of the world of today. His conclusion is that, with exceptions, the Old Testament is not an adequate starting point for showing the significance of idolatry for our times. The most serious aspect is a double assumption. The first is that idols are inane gods, which cannot bring salvation; therefore idolatry is, in the strict sense, stupidity. The second is that idolatry is no longer a phenomenon of the enlightened Western world. But things are not like this. Inanity is not the basic thing about idols; they do, on the contrary, produce victims. And idols exist today in the secular world, perhaps more so than in the Third World.

This basic intuition into idols developed in El Salvador during the years of repression and persecution. I can sum this up as follows: 1. Idols are not a thing of the past or realities that appear only in the religious sphere; they really exist today; they are historical realities that configure society and determine the life and death of most of its members. Archbishop Romero defined and graded them like this: the absolutization of wealth and personal property, the absolutization of national security, the absolutization of organization.[8] 2. These realities are named idols in the strict sense because they present themselves with the characteristics of divinity: ultimateness (one cannot go beyond them), self-justification (they do not need to justify themselves to human beings), untouchability (they cannot be questioned and those who do so are destroyed). 3. The idol by definition, which gives rise to all the others, is the unjust configuration of society, structurally and permanently, and served by many other realities – military, political, patriarchal, cultural, ethnic, judicial, intellectual and

also religious power, which share by analogy in the reality of the idol.
4. These idols demand a cult (the cruel prctices of both capitalism and the
'real socialism' of the past), and they also demand an orthodoxy (the
accompanying ideologies); they promise salvation to those who adore them
(assimilating them to the wealthy and powerful of the First World), but
de-humanize them, 'de-Latin Americanize' them and de-fraternize them.
5. Finally, and most decisively, these idols produce millions of innocent
victims, whom they send to the slow death of hunger, indignity and
insignificance, and to the violent death of repression. The conclusion is
that idols need victims to survive.

Let us return to violence. The violence at source is the idol of injustice –
which in our part of the world, and most others, takes the shape, in the final
analysis, of capitalism, or neo-liberalism. The contribution of liberation
theology is to stress that overcoming violence then means, above all else,
eradicating this idol and raising the struggle to overthrow it to a theological
level: faith in God is at the same time struggle against the idol. And if we
are criticized for always speaking of 'struggle', let me say that this struggle,
which has no need to be bloody, is necessary, and that when believers
allow, tolerate, or take advantage of the idol of capital, then they become
accomplices of the violence that will come later, often bloodily. An analysis
of violence from the viewpoint of idolatry is also important because it
clearly shows that 'fundamentalism' is not just something to do with
religion, in the conventional sense of the term, but with all that 'divinizes'
itself. So capitalism is 'fundamentalist' and it generates aberrant practices.

A little reminder: the essential relationship between the source idol
(wealth, accumulation of capital) and its victims has been very clear in
Latin America from the beginnings. 'Millions of human beings were
sacrificed on the altar of gold and silver. Gold and silver became the new
gods' (Saul Trinidad). 'Why so much violence? . . . Only so that
Christians could realize "their final goal, which is gold"' (Leonardo Boff).
And this is still the case today; as the bishops of Panama put it recently:
'Gold, a god that generated victims. The dollar, an idol that causes death.'

II. Humanizing violence: minimizing evils and maximizing benefits[9]

The idol needs victims if it is to survive and therefore unleashes violence,
its own and that in response. Liberation theology is not ingenuous about
this latter violence, even though it can be legitimate. And it is not in the
least ingenuous about violence overall. It has therefore proposed to
humanize violence, and although the only way to humanize it completely is
to do away with it altogether, we have to put forward ways of humanizing it

while it still exists. In practice, humanizing violence requires a theoretical and practical effort to minimize its evils and, even if this sounds paradoxical, to maximize any benefits that can derive from the occasion of violence.

(*a*) In order to minimize the evils of violence we must first rationalize its use to the fullest degree (in its phase of inevitability and even legitimacy). This is what Ellacuria established with his basic principle of measured response.

> In general, the principle of measured response suggests that cultural benefits should be achieved or defended by cultural means, political ones by political means, religious ones by religious means, and so on. Taking another person's life is in a different dimension from ethnic and cultural, class or political objectives, the more so when conditions exist in which these objectives can be achieved through proportionate means.[10]

This quest to minimize violence by rationalizing its use most fully is the first step – even if it seems a little one, far removed from pacifist utopias – in humanizing it: only in order to defend life and in extreme cases can one do violence to life.

In order to minimize the evil effects of violence, however, even when it may have become legitimate, we also have to struggle against the dehumanizing by-products it produces as a matter of historical fact. In the first place, we have to move beyond the mystique of violence, as denounced time and again by Archbishop Romero. In his third Pastoral Letter of 1976 he wrote: 'Much harm is being done to our people by this fanatical violence that has become almost a "mystique" or "religion" for some groups or individuals. They make violence their god as the sole source of justice and propose and practise it as a means of implanting justice in the country. This pathological mentality makes it impossible to halt the spiral of violence and contributes to the polarization of groups of people.' In the second place, we have to control armed violence strictly so that it never becomes terrorism, defining this as the use of mainly physical violence against defenceless people, civilians or military, with the object of striking terror into them. In the third place, we have to overcome the tendency to militarize every aspect of life, personal and social, and to subordinate any other dimension – economic, social, cultural, trade union, religious, family, personal – to this one. And finally, we have to move beyond the one-sided assumption of ethical superiority – with its accompanying disdain – over those who seek other non-warlike means of struggle and liberation.

The conclusion is simple, but it seems to me decisive: violence produces direct physical evils, but it also tends to produce, indirectly and of necessity, other indirect evils, both physical and moral. Humanizing violence, then, means being honest with reality, recognizing the terrible inhumanity of what violence produces without pushing it out of sight. In any case, what should never be done is to exalt and fall into the mystique of violence.

(b) On the other hand, violence in response, however tragic it may be, can be an expression of love for a people and usually produces positive by-products. This fact – which might be interpreted as analogous with a tragic *felix culpa* – is something recognized and definable, not just a conceptual exacerbation or a despairing attempt to make a virtue out of necessity. The fact is that through and over against its negative side, a positive side also emerges. Let us look at this in three major aspects that have emerged from the conflict in El Salvador.

In the first place, the reality of the situation has made response violence in itself a possible expression of love as a reaction to the terrible source violence. How much the combatants have sought justice and how much they have shown love by opting for the armed struggle with its obvious risks, God alone knows, but we cannot rule out the possibility or deny that the motivation of some or many has been the liberation of their people.

In the second place, violence can be the occasion for the unmasking of lies and calling attention to the truth of a situation. Violence in response is, certainly, violence, but the extent to which it is a *response* to an unhuman situation must also be stressed. Though tragic, then, the violent conflicts are those that have normally made the source violence unmistakable, so that we can begin to take note of its true reality.

Finally, response violence – tragically – expresses the need that exists to go on reacting against injustice; that is, the need to pursue – though in another form – the struggle against injustice. We have to insist on this since at present attitudes of dialogue and tolerance are being proposed; these are necessary and important, but lacking in anything of conflict or conflictive praxis. Historical reality, though, goes on being conflictive and unjust in itself, and therefore we have to keep up the agonistic – struggling – conception that is basic to human existence and to the history of peoples. The steps, small or large, taken by poor people are in no way a gift from the powerful, nor even the product of mere negotiations, but their gain through conflicts and struggles. And this gain, so simple, has to be held on to, since there are those who would eliminate it.

Those countries that have raised up hope as something new, such as Nicaragua and El Salvador in the 1980s, need not only to be destroyed but also discredited and changed into a spurious hope of romantics because they broke the process of homogenization brought in by the Reagan era. The geo-culture of despair and the theology of inevitability today require a global projection to permit the homogenization of the new restructuration promoted by the élite of world power. Despair is the necessary attitude for stability from the ruling standpoint.[11]

Love, truth, the need for struggle and hope are, then, positive qualities of the spirit made present in Central America as a result of conflict. Humanizing violence is not an idealistic thing, but a realistic one, though guided, too, by an ideal: to struggle against and minimize the evils and negative by-products of violence, and to maximize its benefits and positive by-products.

III. Redeeming violence: the martyrs

For liberation theology, the most specifically Christian task is that of redeeming violence. As I said at the beginning, this only happens once it has been eradicated, but to achieve this we have to struggle against it not only from without, but by taking charge of it from within. This – and doing so out of love for the victims – is what the martyrs exemplify. They, and they alone, can overturn the dynamic of violence. This is what Ignacio Ellacuría said in the last article he wrote for *Concilium*, a year before his martyrdom:

It would still seem that from the ultimate Christian standpoint, that of perfection in following the historical Jesus, those Christians who are Christian through and through in their attitudes and actions – while they will be the first and most heroic in fighting all forms of injustice – should not make use of violence. Not that Christians always and everywhere have to reject violence, but Christians acting as such will not normally give their specific witness through the use of violence. This does not mean they leave the 'dirty' work to others, counting themselves among the 'pure' who do not get their hands dirty. It is rather a question of giving the fullest and most comprehensive witness to the fact that life is above death, that love is stronger than hate. Such an approach will always be acceptable and effective, provided that these Christians are prepared to risk even martyrdom in their defence of the poor and struggle against the oppressors through the witness of their words and their life.[12]

With these words Ellacuría sought to express what is most specifically Christian in the face of violence, and also to expound, for possibly more 'bellicose' critics, what might be called an 'apologia' for 'non-armed violence'. So he affirmed three things: 1. that Christians have to be ready to fight against all forms of injustice and to defend the poorest against those who oppress them; 2. that in order to fight they will prefer to use means that in themselves express the supremacy of life over death and of love over hate and 3. that to have credibility in all this Christians have to be 'the foremost and most daring', have to risk 'even martyrdom'.

Ellacuría refers us in the final analysis to openness to martyrdom for justice's sake as the Christian attitude in the face of violence. Here two elements come together, which are in tension and which express the non-simplifying tension of liberation theology in the face of violence: the active struggle against the idol and injustice and the passive acceptance that the idol will react and annihilate.

This fact is clear among us. In El Salvador there are many who, like Jesus, have died martyrs for the kingdom of God. But beyond this fact, these martyrs witness that in order to redeem sin one has to take it upon oneself. A basic affirmation is made in the Old Testament in presenting the suffering Servant of Yahweh and in the New Testament in presenting the crucified Christ. In other words, the old maxim *quod nos est assumptum nos est redemptum* can be applied to sin in general and to violence in particular. In a more modern expression (by René Girard), foundational anti-violent acts are needed to restrain and overturn the pan-violent dynamic of reality.

According to this, Christianity's stance in relation to the eradication of violence is a double one: on the one hand, violence, above all the source violence of injustice, must be combatted from outside with all sorts of arms (very preferably non-military) external to itself; on the other, however, in order to restrain and overturn its originating dynamism, we have to take on violence from within. This is how the cross of Jesus can be interpreted, as Paul seems to do: as an event that overturns the dynamism of violence, since it allows – said in metaphorical words – violence to pour out all its force on Jesus until it is left with no power itself.

So, the martyrs are those who have taken violence upon themselves today. Some have, furthermore, undertaken frontal combat against it through pastoral, trade union, university teaching, and other means, although in the hour of trial these means have not freed them from the death they freely sought. Others have taken it more directly upon themselves – the anonymous martyrs, simple peasants, old folk, women and children above all, massacred with no defences, without even the freedom to flee from death.

How much historical efficacy these martyrs will have in overturning the dynamism of violence is something still to be analysed. But, *a priori* according to Christian faith, we have to state that they are the ones who have taken violence and its sinfulness on themselves. And *a posteriori* we have to say – as witness the case of El Salvador – that they are the ones who have contributed most to hastening the end of armed violence.

Furthermore, though, these martyrs bring to the historical situation they create realities and values opposed to source violence, selfish injustice and cover-up lies, and in this way, like the Servant and Christ crucified, they bring salvation and light. The martyrs are those who bring mercy into a selfish society; those who bring reconciliation into a society of victims and executioners; those who bring justice and peace into an unjust society, one of institutionalized violence. And in the Christian tradition, and in the best common understanding of humankind, the martyrs are those who bring love.

This continues to generate truth, love, justice and hope in history. And this is the dynamism offered to overturn the history of violence and redeem it. This struggling and loving the life of the poor to the end – even if this end turns out to be martyrdom – is what redeems violence in history.

Translated by Paul Burns

Notes

1. According to the latest United Nations report on development, of 17 July 1996, the gap between rich and poor nations is growing in relative terms: in 1990 the proportion was 60 to 1. The wealth of those 385 persons who are each worth more than 1,000 million dollars was greater than the total annual income of 45% of the world's population. In absolute terms, 3,000 million human beings live in inhuman poverty. Eighty-nine countries are worse off than ten years ago, some worse than thirty years ago.

2. Let us just record two facts: 1. The US government sent one million dollars a day to the Salvadorean army, even while it knew of the horrifying massacres this was carrying out; 2. The School of the Americas, directed and financed by the US government, has trained many Latin American military, including some of the most criminal, such as those responsible for the assassination of Archbishop Romero, the members of the Atlacatl battalion who raped and murdered the four US nuns, those who committed the massacre of El Mozote, in which around 1,000 died, mostly women and children, and those who murdered the Jesuits of the UCA and their two women helpers.

3. 'Amnesty International has not ceased pointing out that impunity is the mother of all corruptions, and that when killing is free, temptation to crime becomes habit' (Alfonso Armada in *El País*).

4. The *Spiritual Exercises* of St Ignatius contain a classic text on this exclusive and antagonistic conflictivity inherent in the nature of things. This is the meditation on the two flags, in which he proposes two ways, one of wealth and one of poverty. Both are dynamic, since both lead, by their nature, to other realities: wealth leads to honours,

pride, and all the vices; poverty to opprobrium and contempt, humility, and all the virtues (nn. 142, 146). Each way is clearly exclusive of the other, but St Ignatius insists that they are also antagonistic: 'so that they form three steps: the first, poverty *against* wealth; the second opprobrium or contempt *against* worldly honour; the third, humility *against* pride' (n. 146).

5. For those who might find this surprising, let me recall that Ignacio Ellacuría used to say: 'The ultimate weapon of the church of the poor is holiness.'

6. *Nuestra idea de Dios*, Buenos Aires 1979, 18.

7. Ibid.

8. He saw the first two absolutizations as intrinsically evil. He considered popular organization good and necessary, but capable of turning into an idol if absolutized.

9. What follows in the rest of this article is developed at greater length in my 'Apuntes para una espiritualidad en tempos de violencia. Reflexiones desde la experiencia salvadoreña', in Various, *Iglesia, socidad y reconciliación*, Bilbao 1993, 111–36.

10. I. Ellacuría, 'Violence and Non-Violence in the Struggle for Peace and Liberation', *Concilium* 215, 1988, 76.

11. X. Gorostiaga, 'La mediación de las ciencias sociales y los cambios internacionales', in J. Comblin, J. I. González Faus and J. Sobrino, *Cambio social y pensamiento cristiano en América latina*, Madrid 1992, 131.

12. Ellacuría, 'Violence and Non-Violence' (n. 10), 77.

Women

Excessive Violence against Women in the Name of Religion

Hedwig Meyer-Wilmes

In Western European societies, to talk of violent practices against women in the name of religion means noting the subtle interweaving of religion and culture. This interweaving is evident in the fact that images of women which express an identity with evil (or the devil), their dependence on the male and their passivity, are often supported by the religions. These do not manifest themselves socially simply as religious codes. Thus the heated discussion in the German parliament about the right of women to sexual self-determination in the context of rapes of women in marriage shows that women can claim no legal protection in their homes. Furthermore the verdicts in rape cases continually show how violence inflicted upon women is relativized. For example, it may be suggested that the victim did not offer resistance and left no visible marks of her resistance on the body of the perpetrator. If such an attitude were transferred to other cases, there would be nothing against interpreting a bank robbery as the transfer of money. The murders of children in Belgium have made it clear that the disclosure and prevention of violence against girls has been blocked by 'unholy alliances' of criminals, politicians and the police. These deadly alliances of those in power form a system of violence in a state with a democratic constitution, which can only be stopped by protests from parents, the media, and grass-roots democratic movements. Images of women in our society which make the victims of violence perpetrators (women want it; if a woman says no, she means yes) are on the one hand also communicated by religion and on the other side also criticized, as has been shown by the ecumenical decade of 'The Churches' Solidarity with Women' (1988–1998).

Christian sources for the suppression of women

The religious inculturation of contempt for women is something that Christian women theologians have long criticized, by drawing attention to the fact that an insistence on the father God, the absence of women in positions of church leadership, and the exclusive language of the liturgy, provide ideological and social support for violence done to women. We are afflicted with a legacy of biblical texts which reproduce the whole gamut of sexual violence against women. Sexual denunciation (Dan. 13), coercion (Gen. 12.10; II Sam. 11), extending to rape (Gen. 34; II Sam. 13) and sexual murder (Judg.19), are specific themes. The power of men over women is symbolized in the image of the daughter of Zion, the unfaithful wife, the whore, whose nakedness is uncovered publicly (Ezek. 16.8). A theology of sacrifice and discipleship which refers to the Second Testament, a theology of the suffering of Christ who was 'obedient to death' (Phil 2.8), is commended for imitation by those suffering sexual violence. So behind the theme of the ecumenical decade of 'The Churches' Solidarity with Women' is not just a desire for the integration and recognition of women, but 'a cry for faithfulness to the new community promised in Christ'.[1]

What is violence against women?

At the Fourth World Women's Conference in Beijing in 1995, violence against women was described like this: 'By violence in relations between the sexes we understand any kind of violation of physical and/or mental integrity which is connected with the gender of the victim and the perpetrator and which is exercised by exploiting the balance of power between men and women present in existing structures.'[2] It should be noted that this definition of violence is a consensus formula of the United Nations. One could translate the 'inclusive' language into relationships involving violence by drawing inferences from a statement by a German Protestant women's group: 'Violence against women and girls takes place when they are used against their will by a person (usually a man) to satisfy particular needs. These needs are either of a sexual nature or they are above all non-sexual needs which are expressed in a sexualized form (e.g. the desire to feel powerful, to humiliate, to assert oneself).'[3] The advantage of this definition is its proximity to reality:

Every three minutes a woman is beaten,
every five minutes a woman is raped,
every ten minutes a little girl is molested.
Every day women's bodies are found in alleys and bedrooms,
at the top of the stairs.[4]

We can take this poem by the African American writer Ntozake Shange further: every day children are abused and forced into prostitution; the sexual organs of girls are mutilated; women are burned in India; women and girls are bought and sold; women are gang-raped in war. The scenarios of reality allow only one conclusion: violence against women is part of the everyday life of women all over the world. So the 'gender-neutral' language of the Fourth World Women's Conference is misleading and disguises the actual situation. The perspective indicated in these definitions of violence directs attention to the overall interconnections within the balance of power which lead to the sexual abuse of women. Violence against women is on the one hand branded as structural sin, but on the other hand is distinguished from sexual abuse. This needs explanation: a Catholic statement on violence against women issued within the framework of the ecumenical decade of the churches' solidarity with women shares this perspective of putting sexual violence against women in a wider structure of violence. The male power of definition is included among the structures of violence: 'The pressure to adapt in many spheres of life, the refusal to recognize women's work . . . clerical domination in the church, and the existing form of church structures and ministries.'[5]

Violence is sin

Thus unjust imbalances of power which manifest themselves at various levels are included within the concept of violence: male dominance in making definitions, pressure to adopt the 'female' role, discrimination against 'women's' work and the hierarchical structure of the church. This church structure comprises levels or sub-systems which in the feminist theological debate are referred to as 'kyriarchy', to use a term of Elisabeth Schüssler Fiorenza's. This concept of violence presupposes a fluid transition from 'direct/personal to indirect structural'[6] forms of power. A similar view of the interconnection between forms of violence is also expressed in the final document of the first European Women's Synod (1996). The general interconnection between forms of violence is made concrete here not only with a view to protecting the right to sexual self-determination but also with a view to the economic, political and spiritual situation of women in Europe. 'The fight against poverty is a fight against structural violence': commitment to the ordination of women stands alongside demands for the dismantling of the system of nuclear energy.[7] Various facets of a patriarchal power structure are demonstrated here. This view of violence and relationships coloured by violence is based on the experiences of women in church and society, which tend to regard violence against women as a special case, as an issue for women, and thus to personalize violence (the victim wore a provocative miniskirt; the perpetrator had had a bad childhood).

In the Christian tradition there is an understanding of sin which regards sexuality as the primary locus of sin. Down to our century sexuality has primarily been symbolized in the image of the seductive Eve. From there it was only a small step to the chain of associating sin with sexuality and therefore with woman. Rarely has one heard a clear statement from the church to the effect that 'it is not the experience but the exercise of social toleration of sexual violence that is sin'.[8] Church statements from the sphere of women's pastoral care emphasize that sexual violence is sin because it attacks the physical and mental integrity of a person. It is a sin to abuse trust and power. 'Sexual violence is an attack on God, because it destroys what God has made in God's image.'[9] Those who adopt this position are concerned to reflect not only on the political diagnosis but also on the theological dimension of relationships in which violence is a factor. Talk of structural sin, adopted from liberation theology, is thus transferred to the division of power within society and the church as it relates to violence against women. The question now is how specific sexual violence, as practised in the act of rape and in the sexual abuse of children, can be made a theological theme.

The de-sexualizing of sexuality

In the Protestant's women's definition of violence quoted at the beginning of this article a distinction is made between violence which satisfies needs of a sexual nature and 'non-sexual needs which are expressed in a sexualized form'.[10] This distinction relates to the motive for the misuse of power: force or drive. It is maintained that both these are expressed in a sexualized form. Now I have been struck in the discussion within feminist theology that there is a strong overlap here with the analysis of violence against women. Moreover it seems to me that the sexual is so to speak dissolved in the concept of power. When we talk of rape, sexual harassment, child abuse, pornography and wife-beating, we understand these as instances of violence against women. 'But what seems to be dangerous in this analysis . . . is the assumption that the issue in these questions is violence and not sex: rape is a crime of violence, not a sexual crime; sexual harassment is a misuse of power, not of sexuality; pornography is violence against women and is not erotic.'[11] This warning by the jurist and author Catherine MacKinnon refers to the adoption of a 'male' definition of sexual violence, which understands as illegal only what men understand as illegal. We unintentionally confirm this concept 'when we say that our sexual transgressions stem from misuse of power, not of sex'.[12] Feminist analyses draw a line between sexual intercourse and rape, gestures of affection and sexual harassment, pornography as an artistic depiction and the visual humiliation of women. The battle for women's right to sexual self-determination fought by the women's movement basically consists in the struggle to gain a social acceptance of this demarcation.

However, in the meantime this demarcation has itself become a matter of controversy among feminists. Thus the philosopher Judith Butler regrets that feminists no longer make a distinction between a rape and the visual depiction of a rape. So she regards positions like MacKinnon's as being close to those of right-wing groups and conservative politicians. She insists on the ambivalence of sexuality, which can be both erotic and humiliating. Certainly she does not deny the violence that can be expressed in pictures and words and that traumatizes us socially. But she believes that we could not do away with this social, historical, trauma by constantly repeating how vulnerable we are.[13] Whereas for MacKinnon the problem of sexual abuse lies in the different ways in which men and women perceive sexuality, Butler locates the problem in the ambivalence of sexuality as such. Her vision makes men and women consume gender-variable cosmetics and pornography in the future, whereas MacKinnon wants a situation in which they lie relaxed in the bathtub and read a 'respectable' book together.

Sexual abuse of women is murder of the soul[14]

An 'anonymous' woman describes the consequences of injury by indirect violence like this: 'Where do the words which hurt me when they smashed into me fall? Do I collect them, or what do I do with them? They are not just words; they are energies from body, spirit and soul.'[15] A therapist who works with victims of incest calls her book 'Murder of the Soul'.[16] Women go in search of 'Liberating Images of God for Women',[17] in order to save their souls. The 'anonymous' woman could teach Judith Butler that violent words and images are not only ambivalent but comprise actions which destroy women's bodies. Sexual violence against women is not just a balloon which can be filled at will. I agree with MacKinnon that sexual violence against women must not be neutralized by a reference to situations which involve violence generally. On the other hand I do not think that her 'resexualized' form of the question of power is enough to bring out the violation of sexuality as damage to the person as a whole. The voices of victims of rape show that they regard the violence done to them as a violation of their bodies and souls, i.e. as a violation of their persons.

In the issue of *Concilium* on *Violence Against Women*,[18] Elisabeth Schüssler Fiorenza describes various strategies by which feminist theologians deal with the legacy of the legitimation of violence against women by the Christian religion. One strategy, she says, is to give up the Christian faith which legitimates the violence done to women. Another is to remain a Christian and go on suffering humiliation. However, this impossible alternative between resistance and assimilation does not do justice to the women who understand their process of working through the trauma of violence in a religious way. 'Thus victimized religious women are likely to intensify their search for meaning rather than resort to religious and cultural nihilism.'[19] In other words, traumatic knowledge comprises not only accusation but also 'healing' knowledge or ensouled wisdom.[20] To understand working through experiences of violence as a religious process, even when this implies saying farewell to the God of males, means creating room for other images of God.[21]

Murdering Christ and sacrificing sisters

The feminist debate on christology reflects the attempt to make violence against women, both forms of violence generally and specific violence in particular, a theme, and thus also stop it being theologically tabu. This debate refers to two historical lines of reception for the Christian theology of the cross: one which encourages oppressed men and women to bear the suffering inflicted on them in the name of Christ and another which encourages oppressed men and women to resist the violence done to them. Feminist theologians tend to emphasize the vulnerability of God in Jesus, his presence in the mode of solidarity with the victims.[22] In this conception women's experiences of violence are related to the compassion of Jesus/ God. Suffering, death and violence are not located outside God but in God's relation to creature and creation. Moreover in the logic of this argument Jesus Christ can be understood as 'sister' (Radford Ruether), as 'Miriam's Child, Sophia's Prophet' (Schüssler Fiorenza). But christology becomes a problem where original sin is identified with and symbolized by the female gender and Christ's redemptive action with and by the male gender, in other words, where men have the monopoly of representing Christ and the daughters of Eve have the monopoly of sin.[23]

Women's bodies are raped, burned, mutilated, but they never 'embody' the sacrifice of Christ and the suffering of humankind in the Christian tradition. Women's way of the cross as described by Mary Daly (the burning of widows in India, the mutilation of women's feet in China, the excision of the clitoris in Africa, the burning of witches in Europe, gynaecology in America) pillories the world-wide sexual violence against women as a scandal, not to correlate the suffering of women with the suffering of Christ but to show this up as a perversion of creation and victim. 'Gyn/ecology is de-creation' and re-creation at the same time.[24] De-creation denotes the patriarchal arrangements and superficial distortions in image, action, myth and word which destroy the being of women. Re-creation means recalling 'background' images and 'crone'- ological actions which protect women and preserve their integrity. The outline presented by Elisabeth Schüssler Fiorenza[25] identifies violence against women as a problem on the different levels of Western culture and Christian theology as a question of power. She reconstructs kyriarchal balances of power (violence generally) in connection with Jesus and his discipleship and she 'decontextualizes' this legacy in the interpretative community of 'wo/men-ekklesia'.

The sculptor Christine Kowal Post, who was born in Nigeria, grew up in England and lives in the Netherlands, has carved a statue of a woman out of pinewood. This woman is naked and holds a cup pressed to her body. Her gaze is anxious and expectant, her body sensual and strong. When one walks round the statue one notices that she is concealing a dagger behind her in her left hand. This 'Woman with Cup and Dagger' represents the 'wide limits of permissible violence against women' and the feminist demarcations between violence and sexuality. Her 'nakedness is uncovered', but she is ready to attack. She protects herself with the cup into which the blood of the sacrifice for 'dangerous memory' runs. This woman is the victim, and she is the resistance fighter. She is an image of both damaged and new humanity. A meditation on this image might go like this.

This is my body which I have given for you
a body full of warmth and life
tortured, raped, cold.

This is my blood which I have shed for you
menstrual blood, blood of childbirth, pure blood
flowing, dripping, dead.

This is a weapon which I did not want to use
with cold blade and sharp point.
You have done violence to me
clouded my spirit
hurt my body
made my soul homeless.

Here I wanted only to live, love
believe, hope
become
O God let this cup pass from me.

Translated by John Bowden

Notes

1. A. Gnanadason, 'A Church in Solidarity with Women: Utopia or Symbol of Faithfulness', *Concilium* 1996/1, 74–80: 78.
2. Bundesministerium fur Frauen, Senioren, Familie und Jugend (ed.), 4. *Weltfrauenkonferenz 1995. Beiträge und Positionen der 12 Arbeitsgruppen des Nationalen Vorbereitungskomitees*, Bonn 1995, 7.
3. *Theologische Aspekte der Gewalt gegen Frauen und Mädchen. Stellungnahme der Evangelischen Frauenarbeit in Deutschland*, 1996, 8 (=EFD).
4. Quoted by E. Schüssler Fiorenza, *Violence against Women. Concilium* 1994/2, vii–xxiv: vii.
5. Katholische Arbeitsgruppe in der Ökumenischen Projektgruppe der Ökumenischen Dekade – Solidarität der Kirchen mit den Frauen (1988–1998) (ed.), *Frauen und Mädchen-Gewalt-Kirche*, September 1996, 9 (=KAG).
6. Ibid., 9.
7. Sieth Delhaas et al. (ed.), *Vrouwen bewegen Europa. Verslag-werkboek*, Gorinchem 1996, 189–93.
8. KAG, 17.
9. Ibid.
10. EFD, 8.
11. Catherine MacKinnon, 'Gewalt gegen Frauen in neuer Sicht', in Barbara Schaeffer-Hegel (ed.), *Frauen und Macht. Der alltägliche Beitrag der Frauen zur Politik des Patriarchats*, Berlin 1984, 229–37: 229.
12. Ibid., 235.
13. Interview with Judith Butler, 'We zijn allemaal kwetsbaar in de publiek ruimte', *Filosofie Magazine* 5, 1996, 9, 36–8.
14. The title refers to the remark of a rape victim, Theresia Brechmann, 'Vergewaltigung ist Mord an der Seele', *Sexualpädagogik und Familienplanung der Pro Familia* 11, 1983, 2, 2–5, and her book *Jede dritte Frau. Protokoll einer Vergewaltigung*, Reinbek bei Hamburg 1981/1987.
15. Quoted in KAG, 10.
16. Ursula Wirtz, *Seelenmord. Inzest und Therapie*, Stuttgart 1989.
17. Annie Imbens-Fransen, *Befreiende Gottesbilder für Frauen. Damit frühe Wunden heilen*, Munchen 1997 (Dutch 1995).
18. *Concilium* 1994/2.
19. Ibid., xix.
20. Cf. Hedwig Meyer-Wilmes, *Zwischen lila und lavendel. Schritte feministischer Theologie*, Regensburg 1996, 110–17.
21. Thus the pastoral worker Annie Imbens-Fransen points out that women who have grown up with a patriarchal image of God have difficulties not only in coping with violent experiences but also in speaking of God positively (see n. 17 above).

22. Thus e.g., Julie Hopkins, *Towards a Feminist Christology*, Kampen 1994, 55–63.

23. Cf. Jacqulyn Grant, *White Women's Christ, Black Women's Jesus*, Atlanta 1989, 144.

24. Mary Daly, *Gyn/Ecology. The Metaethics of Radical Feminism*, Boston 1978, 424.

25. Elisabeth Schüssler Fiorenza, *Jesus. Miriam's child, Sophia's Prophet. Critical Issues in Feminist Christology*, New York and London 1995.

The Role of Women in Overcoming Violence

Mary Grey

I. Christ and violence against women

A man in the last moments of his life, undergoing torture and appalling humiliation, responds to the compassion of the daughters of Jerusalem (Luke 23.28) by pouring out his own compassion and prophetic insight on what was and would continue to be the tragic situation of women through the ages – violence legitimated by civilization and religion alike. Compassion, sensitivity to the suffering of women and judgment on the systems which kept it in existence was a consistently strong feature of the ministry of Jesus of Nazareth. He refused to condemn the adulterous woman (John 7); he forgave the prostitute who anointed his feet (Luke 7.36–50); he showed consistent compassion for the isolation and poverty of widows (Luke 7.11–17; 21.1–4); and the first words of the risen Jesus to a woman were a response to her sorrow, 'Woman, why do you weep?' (John 20.15). Here, then, are sufficient grounds for hope that violence in the name of religion is not the last word: to be mined from the tradition are resources for healing and transformation.

That was the conviction of the international group of women theologians who gathered at San José in Costa Rica, December 1994, at the invitation of the Women's Commission of EATWOT (Ecumenical Association of Third World Theologians).[1] We believed that religion was both part of the problem and part of the solution and that, as women in theology, we had a responsibility to take action.[2]

1. Naming sources of violence in religious traditions.

So the first step was to name the violence and its sources, specifically where religion must take responsibility. Especially important was the naming of the interconnections of many forms of violence – cultural and ecological, domestic and sexual, economic and military violence – in their contextually specific forms. Violence against women is named now in changing times when some churches have in fact begun to name it, and to begin to initiate some form of action, however minimal and inadequate to the extent of the situation.[3]

But when it comes to naming the religious sanctioning of violence, reluctance to speak the truth reigns. Even if culturally, through the work of René Girard, there is a tacit understanding that violence underlies the whole logic of civilization – and always has done – yet the deep-rooted connection of this logic with violence against women is seldom acknowledged.[4] Naming the sources of violence in our religious traditions means naming the sources which continuously demean women's sexuality and legitimate male violent expressions of this. For example, the story of the concubine in Judges 19, raped, murdered, her body cut into twelve pieces, in a biblical context of escalating violence, has to be named and condemned as violence against women: only as such can it be the liberating word of God.[5] The links have to be made with the continuing sanctioning of the rape of women in war – as in the recent atrocities in Bosnia. The frequent portraying of women by scripture and tradition – across all religions – as not possessing full human subjectivity, but only derivatively so, as possession of husband or father, has to be recognized as a contributory cause of domestic violence. Women as property of men are vulnerable to battering, dowry murder, even to becoming commodities as trafficking in women's bodies increases. This is all occurring in contexts where degraded expressions of sexuality have become the norm, where violence against women occurs within new forms of colonialism and is increased by racist discrimination against Afro-Caribbean, Hispanic and Asian women. The work needing to be done by men in confronting the causes of their own violence has scarcely begun; it is clear that povery, lack of clear identity, hopelessness, are all contributory factors to men beating their wives in many cultures: deeper still is the fear of the uncontrollability and irrationality of sexuality which underpins some of the projections of women as being the carnal other; and while the struggle against poverty is genuinely engaged with by churches and faith communities, the failure of the churches to name the links between its male authority figures, the abuse of power, and violence against women and children is a glaring failure. Religion similarly fails to name its own responsibility for the socializing of women into accepting cultural norms which sanction violence.

Thus, whereas Christianity focuses on mercy and compassion for the weak, it continues to ideologize suffering in a way which leaves no window of hope for the beaten wife who cannot leave a violent husband. The central doctrine of salvation, the atonement, continues to proclaim redemption through suffering, sacrifice and expiation, thus sanctioning the trapped woman in a violent relationship because she is sharing the sufferings of Christ.[6] Holiness is still related to endurance of hardship and suffering, and seldom to the celebration of life in its fullness.

2. Standing in effective solidarity

Naming leads to action, an action which opens up the path of resistance, change and the refusal of violence from the disastrous interpretations in the sources of religious faith. The urgency of the moment is the fact that women are suffering and in danger of being killed now. We cannot wait for more books to be written, synods to be summoned, the long process of conversion to be completed. Women have to be rescued now. Building on the commitment to justice for all human beings which is at the core of religion, for Christian churches this means recognizing that we do not yet possess the right structures: the rape shelters, the refuges and the economic support do not usually come from church sources, which are so geared to preserving the family at all costs. So we have to work with whatever organizations are really addressing the situation.[7] But we also have to work both globally and locally: even if one issue is taken seriously – for example, the trafficking in women – it is clear that this affects more than one region and that effective solidarity has to make all the connections possible, in order to eradicate root causes. Child prostitution may be rife in Thailand and the Philippines, but it is Europe and America from which the tourist agencies originate. But if religion does not yet contain effective structures for the eradication of violence, what are its resources which can be tapped?

3. Reclaiming prophetic anger

Prophetic anger, from Moses to Amos, from Micah to Jesus of Nazareth, has railed against injustice in the name of the great vision of the reign of God, the kingdom of peace and justice. Yet here we are reclaiming what the prophets do not name. Amidst the eloquent pleas to those 'who trample on the needy, and bring the poor of the land to an end' (Amos 8.4); the condemnation of those who have forsaken God in idolatry, 'the fountain of living waters . . . for broken cisterns' (Jer. 2.13), and who ignore the plight of the fatherless and the widow (Isa. 1.23b), there is a total blindness with reference to violence against women. Adultery is used as a metaphor for the faithless Israel (Hos. 2–3), which has given weight to the negative sexual stereotyping of women. Only in the book of Daniel do we have the condemnation of lying about a woman, Susanna, and the wrongful accusation of adultery; but this is more a story of the wisdom of Daniel than the vindication of Susanna (Daniel 13). Similarly, the wrath of God is roused frequently against sinful Israel, even if God does not give vengeful expression to this (Hos. 11.11). But it seems that God is not angry at the violation of the concubine, at the sacrifice of Jephthah's daughter, at the rejection of Hagar. Yet if God's anger is a biblical metaphor of judgment on sin, then we have to claim it now as condemnation of violence against women. Prophetic discernment moves on to name and condemn every sin against unjust relation as totally abhorrent within the vision of the reign of God. God is worshipped as God of justice, whose passion is for right relation, who knows about vulnerability, and who is the protector of the weak. This is the liberating word which must now be proclaimed. In the name of this word we have to take courage into our hands to reject the texts which are not liberating, and to use prophetic imagination with texts which are, but which do not name violence against women. Prophetic imagination moves on and addresses specific contemporary needs. Thus Stella Baltazar, from an Indian context, reclaims the Martha/Mary text (Luke 10.38–42) frequently used to keep women in crippling servitude:

> When we try to lift the patriarchal veil from this passage, we see a dynamism from where Jesus usually emerges. The dichotomizing of action and contemplation, that contemplation is the better position, that Martha seems to stand condemned before Mary: all these are assumptions arising from this domination model of scriptural interpretation. It is the task of women to free Jesus from the patriarchal hold and allow him to be an ordinary man who was involved with Martha and Mary as friends.[8]

Again, the biblical Hagar, used and abused by both Sarah and Abraham, is now reclaimed as prophetic inspiration for black womanist communities in the USA.[9] The Ghanaian theologian Mercy Amba Oduyoye writes that 'African women live by a spirituality of resistance which enables them to transform death into life and to open the way to a reconstruction of a compassionate world'.[10] At the beginning of the decade of Churches in Solidarity with Women, referring to the stone which blocks the experience of the Risen Christ, she has also declared that women themselves will roll away the stone of oppression which has lain on them for centuries.[11]

4. Commitment to ongoing conversion

To be effective, naming the sources, standing in solidarity, reclaiming prophetic anger and imagination must stand firmly within faith communities committed to conversion. Conversion represents the core of Christian faith: it is the nodal point where the sin of violence, because it infects every area of our common life, must stand at the heart of the conversion process.

There is now a dawning realization that faith communities, like being a recovering alcoholic, a recovering racist, must always be engaged on a journey of recovery from endemic violence. The task – which divides both along gender and cultural lines – is indeed daunting, but every context dictates its specificity. In the north, the focus required is both our refusal to collude any longer in keeping vicious economic systems in place – which are frequently racist forms of neo-colonialism – forcing the peoples of the south into destitution and our commitment to eradicating all forms of sexual violence and the degradation of sex in our own context.

There is a gender distinction in the journeys of conversion to be undergone: women must examine our own complicity in violent systems, in violence against our own bodies, or the way we collude in violence against other women, often in a racist manner. Men have to address urgently the links between power, violence and the construction of their own identity. The fact that the manhood of Jesus manifests compassion and tenderness; that Jesus weeps publicly; that he opts for the healing of lepers, a haemorrhaging woman, vulnerable children, and nowhere manifests a macho dimension, and that the most admired of his followers do the same – this is a resource to be reclaimed. In all our contexts, any Christian teaching which has been interpreted to condone violence must be expunged.

But the work of analysis cannot be done on behalf of the victims of violence: the task is always to listen and learn how victims of violence themselves want to be empowered, need solidarity, and how they are already acting as their own agents in the process, as well as to become aware that in numerous networks women of all faiths and of no explicit faith commitment across the world are already acting in solidarity to resist violence.

It seems that – at least before the coming of the kingdom – the work of conversion will never come to an end: every hour, relentlessly, there is yet another manifestation, yet one more link uncovered in the complicity of our civilization in the complex logic of violence.

5. Empowered by ritual

The task is indeed formidable – but religion also offers practical sources of healing through ritual. At the dialogue at Costa Rica referred to earlier, despite the painful nature of the discussions, the rituals were transforming experiences. But if Christianity sincerely believes this, if the church as a whole wants to be part of the healing and not the destructive process, then the language of ritual urgently claims attention. If liturgy is to heal from violence, the violence of exclusion through exclusive language needs urgent action. Women cannot be healed if our presence is not acknowledged.

Secondly, if the style of worship is not inclusive and non-hierarchical, then abuse which is itself caused by damaged expressions of power cannot be addressed. But what is more important than style is that the place and space of worship itself is safe and not itself a place of fear. This asks for a process of trust-building as a precondition for healing ritual and for trust-building relationships to be an inclusive part of the ritual itself. Ritual can be healing because it may, for the first time, be a place of breaking the silence which surrounds violence against women. Ritual has the power – in the name of the assembled *ecclesia* – to proclaim violence as totally abhorrent to the law of love, to the Christic paradigm where priority is given to the poorest and weakest, and to the justice of the kingdom of God.

For too long our worship has privileged the word to the exclusion of the body. For too long it has failed to engage the whole person, body, spirit and heart, in the process of healing and conversion. And yet, eucharistic worship is first and foremost about re-membering. The point here is that through re-membering Christ's table fellowship and his final meal which recalled God's saving action in liberating the suffering children of Israel from Pharaoh, violated and broken women can be re-membered. The dry bones of the prophecy to Ezekiel are re-membered as the bodies of the victims of violence, who are mourned in our eucharistic fellowship: but the promise of the new breath of the Spirit given to the prophet is claimed as the hope given to *living* women and children of the community's resistance, its determination to put an end to violence.

Eucharistic worship touches the deepest sacramental imagination. If blood symbolizes – in this context – abuse and violation, the bread of life is the most fundamental symbol of survival.[12] Chung Hyun Kyung, the Korean theologian, told – at the Costa Rica dialogue – the terrible story of the Korean comfort woman, Soo Bock, who, unlike many of her companions, abused by the Japanese soldiers, chose to eat.[13] Eating was both a gesture of resistance and a choice for survival. Stories of prison confinement, torture and war situations abound where the sharing of a piece of bread kept alive hope not just for survival, but for surviving as human beings. Not only are solidarity, hope and love expressed sacramentally through eating, but anointing takes on renewed sacramental significance. Normally seen as symbolizing the gift of the Holy Spirit, anointing here also symbolizes concretely the healing powers of oil for abused and violated bodies. It symbolizes the restoration of dignity and humanity to humiliated women. It evokes the imagination and hope that women and men will discover their bodies as the means of experiencing mutuality and compassion, instead of as instruments of domination or oppression.

Finally, what religions offer are a vision of existence restored and renewed. As we approach the millennium, the dismal discourse of

apocalyptic gloom is frequently heard: the four riders of the Book of
Revelation are on the move, we are told. But, in Christianity, the vision of
the restoration of relationships, that great kin-dom of right relation
between women, children, men and creation kept before our eyes both in
worship and in daily struggles, is what nourishes hope that the logic of
violence will not have the last word. Not apocalypse now, but commitment
to the basic story of Christianity, right relation and justice for the most
vulnerable, is what nourishes our courage, our quest and our life in
common.

Notes

1. The book which resulted from this dialogue is *Women Resisting Violence:
Spirituality for Life*, ed. Mary John Mananzan, Mercy Amba Oduyoye, Elsa Tamez,
J. Shannon Clarkson, Mary C. Grey and Letty M. Russell, Maryknoll 1996.
2. Participants came from every continent: the process was coordinated by Mary
John Mananzan, Letty Russell, Mary Grey and Elsa Tamez, who was responsible for
hospitality in Costa Rica.
3. Aruna Gnanadason, *No Longer Secret*, Geneva 1993; National Board of Catholic
Women, London, *Raising Awareness of Domestic Violence*; Women's Inter-Church
Council of Canada, *Hands to End Violence against Women: A Handbook for Theological
Education*, Toronto 1988; Bulletin of *Femme et Hommes dans L'Eglise*, Paris; Fiona
Hulbert (ed.), Bulletin of EFECW, 93/94, Brussels, *Structural Violence*; *Breaking the
Silence on Violence against Women*, Network of Ecumenical Women in Scotland,
Dunblane 1994.
4. See Gil Bailie, *Violence Unveiled: Humanity at the Crossroads*, New York 1995.
5. It is named by Phyllis Trible, 'An Unnamed Woman: the Extravagance of
Violence', in *Texts of Terror*, Philadelphia 1984, 65–91.
6. This is despite much feminist theological writing which makes the connections
clear and calls for different interpretations of atonement. See Joann Carlson Brown and
Carole Bohn (eds.), *Christianity, Patriarchy and Abuse*, Ohio 1989; M. Grey,
Redeeming the Dream, London 1989.
7. In England this means, for example, Womankind Worldwide, World in Action
etc.
8. Stella Baltasar, 'Domestic Violence in Indian Perspective', in *Women Resisting
Violence* (n. 1), 61.
9. See Dolores Williams, *Sisters in the Wilderness: the Challenge of Womanist God-
Talk*, Maryknoll 1993.
10. Mercy Amba Oduyoye, 'A Spirituality of Reconstruction and Resistance', in
Women Resisting Violence (n. 1), 162.
11. Mercy Amba Oduyoye, *Who Will Roll the Stone Away?*, Geneva 1988.
12. There can be no quick leap here to the 'redeeming blood of the Cross of Christ'.
This has functioned for so long to keep women enduring violence: the healing qualities
of Jesus's mission and ministry are what need stressing.
13. See Chung Hyun Kyung, 'Your Comfort versus My Death', in *Women Resisting
Violence* (n. 1), 129–40.

Dissidents

Between Violence and Dialogue: The Religions in the Twentieth Century

Andrea Riccardi

I. The decline of religion?

The twentieth century began and developed in an atmosphere of crisis for the religions. Some people argued that the religions would not last the century. The cultural climate led them to think that in the modern world the role of the religions and faith in the life of individuals and society would be much reduced. This conviction was shared by believers themselves: some hailed modernity as a force which would purge religious faith of its human dross; others argued that faith would inevitably be limited to the sphere of conscience. Yet others resigned themselves to the death-throes of the religions, believing that faith would nevertheless survive in people's hearts in unforeseeable ways.

It was thought that faith would no longer make a mark on society and its institutions, but become an interior matter. The discussions of these forecasts divided religious leaders: should they put up stubborn opposition to a modernity which was eating away faith or should they accommodate to it by bringing the world of religion up to date? This has been an eternal debate, and in it the two positions are not as far removed from each other as appears at first sight. In the twentieth century Catholicism, to focus on one organized religion, opted for intransigent opposition to modernity yet did not reject moments and areas of adaptation (or *aggiornamento*, as Vatican II put it).

However, this century has indeed eroded the religious sphere, to such a degree that the practice of worship and religious rites has undergone a sharp decline. Our century also developed a view of the world and the state which established their autonomy from the claims of the religions to make total sense of them. From the French Revolution on, secularization and modernity have been conceived as a utopia bringing liberation from obscurantism and fanaticism, by means of a freer and more authentic view of life. The state's view has been a secular one, and the secular view has even been an ethic that has become as it were a lay religion, with its own social rites. The secular state has eroded the social role of the religions while affirming, in the equality of citizens before the state, religious freedom for any faith and any opinion. Society has ceased to identify itself with a religion.

Has this not been the most balanced form of social life, which has reduced the monopoly of the religious? Twentieth-century Europe is convinced of this, even if its conversion in the direction of secularization has been very slow, because of the persistence of links between state and religion. It is so convinced of this that it has convinced the religious. Thus at the heart of the twentieth century, its main religion, Catholicism, proclaimed in its solemn council that religious freedom is also a sacred value. Furthermore Europe believes that the secular view is something to export, part of the package of our civilization. However, outside the confines of Europe, in the Mediterranean basin, the only example of a secular state is Ataturk's Turkey. In Europe itself the secular state has not been a vision which is shared by all; that was the case not only in Franco's Spain but even more in Communist Eastern Europe. Is secularity a universal value?

Communism – another decisive factor of our twentieth century – shares the current view of religion and takes it to extremes. The modern socialist world, once it had been fully achieved, was to make religion disappear. Communism is basically the last great Western utopia which is considered to be a message at a universal level, good for every latitude. Communism constructed a state which was profoundly different from the secular Western state, because the Communist state is to some degree confessional in its anti-religious character; it has a state position on religious matters, atheism, which is reflected in the struggle with religion. The Communist state is a theological state, atheistic in essence, but following the type of the confessional state.

Twentieth-century Europe has secular states, while society is becoming more secular. Moreover Judaism, too, recognizes the primacy of the emancipated and secularized Jewish world: the state of Israel was created more by secular Zionism than by religious Zionism. For Islam, Western culture forecast a similar process to that in Europe, in which religion would become a private matter and – for the ignorant masses – an instrument of control. Also in the Arab world, the motive force towards modernization seemed to be the nationalistic drive which embraced Islam, as for the liberal and nationalistic middle classes elsewhere it embraced Christianity. Religion went down well with the ignorant masses who were not emancipated: it represented a transition towards civilization. The secular structure of Turkey, backed up with armed force, appeared to be a model of development for the whole of the Islamic world, despite the fact that the masses in Anatolia were still steeped in religious faith. The Iran of the Shah was another similar model which the West looked at with interest. Moreover the modernization of Tunisia or Arab nationalist socialism seemed to bring religion within a framework of strong political control, in such a way as to make it an instrument for controlling the masses of people.

II. The 'divine surprise'

The twentieth century continued with the idea that modernity was sweeping religion away from its role as a protagonist in history. This view was considered to be civil process: religion came to be associated with fanaticism or with the memory of the wars of religion which had stained Europe with blood or which had been fought between the Christian world and the Muslim world. The elimination of religion from social life was regarded as a factor of progress and stability. This view, deeply assimilated by Western secular culture, found its most schematic expression in Marxism, where the realization of the socialist society implied the end of the religions considered as a clear regressive element. Modernity had prevailed over religion, which seemed to be a left-over from yesterday's view of the world. Sociologists and politicians, scholars and economists, were substantially in agreement here.

The 1970s proved to be the time of the 'divine surprise'. Religion of every kind reappeared as a relevant factor in the political life of many countries of the world. The religions became an element of stability or instability, of war or peace. This happened even before the crisis of the Marxist ideology, the end of which accentuated the phenomenon. However, there is no need to revive the ghost of the wars of religion, as is often done: neither faith nor theology make people fight, although the religious aspect is by no means a secondary factor in the stability or instability of so many situations. Some argue that the wars of religion must be met with the preaching of tolerance and education towards a secular world. Nevertheless, the religions have revived where secularity had been preached or imposed, even where an anti-religious line had been imposed.

The appearance of the religions as a relevant factor is a complex process which merits an intelligent examination. It should not be exploited, if the raising of ghosts in order to create conflicts is to be avoided. First of all, it is a fact that relates to all the religious worlds, whether Jewish, Christian or Muslim, though differently in different areas. In the Christian world, despite the crisis for the Catholic Church caused by Western secularization, a season of new political and social activity opened up with the election of John Paul II, the first Slavonic pope in the history of Catholicism. The day after his election, this pope sent out a message to Christians, 'Have no fear.' The time had come for the idea of the presence of Christianity in society. Beyond the assessments of the role of the Polish crisis and therefore of Catholicism in the changes in the Soviet bloc, it has been noted how the church became the motive force behind pressure from part of civil society without ever reaching a breaking point which could have provoked Soviet intervention in Poland. The Catholic Church in Poland, in a situation of severe social pressure, took over the role of the opposition. Beyond question John Paul II and the Polish crisis form a situation in which the religious factor, with peaceful social pressure, managed to become an element in destabilizing as great an empire as that of the Soviet Union. The role of Orthodox religious dissent in the USSR was far less, but it too must not be played down.

However, the phenomenon is not limited to the East. In Latin America, liberation theology, a current of thought and a way of organizing the base communities which developed among Catholics, has shown a concern for new social action on the part of Christians. These communities did not accept the social and political *status quo* but theorized on the change with marked attention to revolutionary and Marxist practices. This is a very different position from that of John Paul II, but it is also a symptom of Catholicism as a relevant social factor. A new role for Christianity appeared in Africa: we might think of the Anglican archbishp and Nobel prizewinner Desmond Tutu, who became a symbolic figure in the struggle against apartheid. Moreover – and this is a phenomenon which began in the 1980s – the episcopates or individual bishops became points of reference in the transition between regimes: they represented a political presence while the African state was in crisis.

The West recognized the social and political power of Islam and Khomeini's revolution in 1979. In fact the Western policy, especially in its colonial form, had been clear that the religious feeling of the Muslim population must not be provoked. However, in Iran the situation was very different: a Westernizing regime which had controlled religion, keeping it at a low level, was replaced by a revolutionary regime which used Islam as an element for destabilizing the solid power of the Pahlevis. After Khomeini, the world discovered the reality of Islamic fundamentalism, forgetting that the phenomenon was much older, as could be seen from the episode of the Egyptian Muslim Brotherhoods in the middle of the century. Moreover a crisis developed for Arab nationalisms: the nation state could not always control unsettled and contradictory societies. There was a crisis not only for nationalism but also for socialism, which had spread widely in the Arab world and in the southern hemisphere. This is not the place to take up the topic of Islamic fundamentalism; my sole concern is to emphasize the relationship which came to be established between Islamism and the reality of what in the 1960s Frantz Fanon called the *Wretched of the Earth*. These worlds of wretchedness and exclusion had found in Marxism and in the revolutionary ideologies an instrument for asserting themselves in their own regions. Islamism found room to move and open questions.

In the strategic considerations of the West, fundamentalism is regarded as a strong destabilizing force and is preoccupying Western observers. The interpretative scheme that has been used for Islam, modelled on that typical of Christianity, has proved fragile: it is not possible to separate religion and society in Islam as it is in Christianity. Moreover, there is also a profound difference in the origins of the two religions: Islam arose as both a religion and a society, whereas Christianity arose as a minority religion and remained so for at least three centuries; moreover it was persecuted by the state. Furthermore the separation of religion and society, typical of secular Western regimes, does not work with Judaism either. Most recently in Israel we have seen the assertiveness of religious parties and their direct involvement in political questions. Here too is an element of that 'divine surprise' represented by the phenomena of recent years: the return of God, or better the return of the religions, as protagonists in political and social life.

III. The religions as a disruptive factor

Now it has been noted that the religions can be a disruptive factor, sometimes leading to violence. The religions do not represent just the world of conservation which is naturally bound up with the old regime; they can also represent protest and reaction against the existing order, as an aspiration towards the new. Hence the link between extreme forms of religion and terrorism. The field of so-called fundamentalism is opening up as a phenomenon which cuts across all the religious communities, but its particular features and the dangers it poses differ, depending on the country and the religious system of reference. I believe that the extreme and violent forms of religion preserve a link with the background from which they have come or to which they make reference, at least a link with the breeding ground from which they draw their energy. The religions themselves can do much to channel or prevent the development of extreme forms within them if – as the majority of religious leaders assert – the presuppositions of their own faith do not motivate actions of an extreme kind.

I have been led to look beyond the religious extremism which can take on mass aspects and not just be represented by small groups, and to consider religion as a popular factor. With the crisis of the ideologies, religion is once again becoming a prime element of national identity. That could be seen in the conflict in former Yugoslavia, where the identification of the Croats with Catholicism and the Serbs with Orthodoxy had serious results: it also led to a re-Islamicization of the Bosnians, whose religious features had been deeply eroded. This is not religious extremism, nor are there the phenomena of a religious war (that category cannot be used to explain any of today's scenes of conflict). Nevertheless, the various religious identities which have long existed side by side in a secular state represent a focal point of hostility and justification for the struggle. Often, as is clear from the case of Serbia, the religious element, i.e. Serb Orthodoxy, has a far more national and nationalistic political view than that of the leaders of the country.

We could survey all the conflicts which the religious element tends to accentuate: from that in Armenia/Azerbaijan through Russia/Chechnya, to the Lebanon, the Sudan and the Middle East. In the Christian countries, religion is reappearing as a strong factor of identity which also provides legitimation. That has been evident during the time of the Russian president Boris Yeltsin, in a country where the basic stratum of Holy Russia is strong, but where there are also other prominent religious communities. The Orthodox Patriarch, Alexis II, presided over a ceremony which was a symbol of the rediscovery of Russian religious identity. The religions are returning as a phenomenon of mass identity. It is an ambiguous phenomenon, because in Eastern Europe – see Poland – important signs of de-Christianization have become evident since the victory of the Catholic Church in 1989. However, it is a general fact that in the disintegration of society and the crisis of identity, the religions are proving to be a factor in identity, if not a civil factor.

Now, at the end of the twentieth century, it seems that the course of a century of secularization has been given the lie by the 'divine surprise'. Do we need to consider the religions as factors leading to backwardness and fanaticism? I believe that this is a partial and negative interpretation. The religions represent a complex world of believing men and women, of values, and of a rich experience of profound social depth. Like any important factor in human history, the religions can present different and contradictory aspects and can contribute to both stability and instability. On the other hand, the religious phenomenon must not be absolutized: the religious worlds are important in some areas of the world, but are not always determinative. The great facts of modern history are the result of a combination of different factors which include religion.

IV. The positive function of the religions

The religions are not just an element of conflict or tension. If they are, this is only to a marginal degree. The positive function of the religions in society does need to be examined, but this is not my task. Nevertheless, I think that in the great cities of the world, in districts overcrowded as a result of urbanization, religious identity represents an important link for scattered and anonymous men and women. This dispersion and anonymity are often the sphere in which dangerous developments take place or criminal forces assert themselves. The religions are often the points of reference for a network of social solidarity which is very important for people. The religious rebirth which can be noted in so many countries and so many religious traditions – but not in all of them everywhere – is closely connected with the anthropological crisis of contemporary men and women. Our world has adopted Westernized models of life, but many areas – indeed the majority of areas – have not reached the level of life in the West.

Here we have a topic which I cannot touch on, namely the role of religious identity as an important factor in the staying power of secular society itself. But this stayng power is a combination of many factors: we cannot think of a modern society in a monistic and thus also in a religious way without its becoming totalitarian and violent. However, its complexity is also based on the presence of the religious factor. In a great many countries, secularization has not abolished the space of religion (even if it has reduced it), but has secularized the wider framework of social life. To take Italy as an example. In the 1950s it was still a profoundly Catholic society; it underwent a process of marked secularization in the 1970s and 1980s; but religion has not disappeared, even if society has become profoundly secularized. In Italy the average number of churchgoers on a Sunday (and for Catholics, to attend mass on Sunday is a religious obligation) is a little below 30%, and that is one of the highest in Europe. Religion has not disappeared, but society has become secularized. Has this phenomenon happened in the countries on the south shore of the Mediterranean? Or has the process of re-Islamicization swept away secularization? I do not believe so: in the modern world the rebirth of religion no longer radically sweeps away the secularized framework of reference in the modern world.

V. The beginnings of religious universalism

In the twentieth century, the religious world has undergone an important development: as befits its message, it has become more universalistic. In other words, the religions do not just break barriers and lead to conflicts: they can be an element of social and international stability, contributing towards understanding rather than opposition. I do not mean here to emphasize the role of social cohesion which the religions can have, but above all the international aspect and its connection with the prevention of conflicts. Here we have the problem of the relationship between religion and nation, which is one of the most fascinating chapters in modern history. Religion – though here Judaism differs – always looks towards a wider whole, the *umma* of believers or the universal church, beyond the confines of the individual nation state. The person who is other from a nationalistic perspective remains a member of the same religion from a religious perspective: how can my brother be my enemy? Nationalism and religious universalism gave political and religious leaders a hard time in the years of the World Wars, so much so that a novelist was led to ask with which of the armies of God's faithful God was fighting. Certainly religious universalism is in tension with national identity and national interests. If the religious organizations – and here I am thinking of the Islamic organizations – do not always have the capacity to prevent conflicts, they can certainly educate people not to feel enemies to one another. Nationalism and religion is a problem today in Eastern Europe, where Orthodoxy presents a morphological difference from Catholicism by virtue of its capacity to rediscover itself in the framework of national identity, not least through the system of autocephaly.

By their very nature and mission, the central religious institutions have a vision which goes beyond national confines. In this century as never before, a supranational institution like the Roman papacy is developing an explicit commitment to peace. The pope of Rome is the typical example of a supranational institution which presents itself as an element of communication between the peoples. But this is not the only case. The Ecumenical Patriarchate of Istanbul, especially since the election of Athenagoras I in 1948 (but in some respects also in the first decades of the twentieth century), is a similar case.

1948 saw the creation of the World Council of Churches, which the majority of the Protestant and Orthodox churches joined, but not the Catholic Church. Its universalistic function is clear, and this has led it to deal with some critical and tense situations. Here is another example of the growth of religious commitment and the awareness of a capability to be a factor of peace or war. The very growth of this commitment can be registered in the different national religious communities. Nor should the role of the Jewish dispersion in the West be neglected as a moderating element and not just support for Israeli policy – though this is a very specific instance, one above all related to the state of Israel.

Another characteristic aspect of recent decades in the religious field has been the dialogue between the great religious communities. Here the universalistic elements led not only beyond national boundaries but even beyond religious frontiers. The religious dialogue has developed within the Christian tradition itself: it is ecumenism between Catholics, Orthodox, Pre-Chalcedonians and Protestants. But beyond question the most interesting chapter has been the relationship between the great religious traditions like Judaism, Christianity and Islam. The usefulness of this dialogue is open to discussion: one can ask whether it does not represent a courageous *avant-garde* activity which has not succeeded in reaching the convictions or minds of the mass of believers. However, it must be noted that processes of change in the religious mentality are very slow and take generations.

Dialogue is a distinctive feature of the traditional heritage of the religions, even if it has undergone marked development in the twentieth century. Islam, which is represented as an intolerant religion, can in fact look back on a history of cohabitation with other religious committees. The history of Islamic tolerance, which cannot be resumed now in the forms it took in the past, represents a significant feature, not least by comparison with the Christian world in past centuries, which was intolerant and in which there was no space for the religious minorities. Ottoman society was a multi-religious regime, for all its asperities. Intolerance is not inscribed on the chromosomes of Islam. Moreover Islamic theology itself give a religious status to Christians and Jews.

A far-reaching *aggiornamento* has also taken place in the Christian churches. Vatican II offered a theological vision for the religious other, in particular for Jews and Muslims. Its key point is the transition from the figure of the infidel to that of the believer who belongs to another religion, who is not just respected because he or she represents another social reality but is also understood in his or her religious perspective. Furthermore, the great religions with a missionary and universalistic vocation which have directed their missions all over the world have experienced that peoples do not 'convert' to their faith (or do so only partially). The world does not embrace, and does not seem likely ever to embrace, a single religious faith: this fact is forcing the religions to ask themselves about the need to live together, to engage in dialogue and to understand one another. Reality and the religious traditions have constantly given rise to a demand for dialogue and undersanding between the different religious worlds. This orientation contrasts with the tendency to retreat into a narrow identity and to engage in conflict, and with the use of the religions for nationalistic or bellicose ends. In this sense the religious communities (whose morphologies and attitudes to faith are very different), are having to make some choices. They are being driven to deepen their own religious traditions, and to establish new relations with others.

Translated by Mortimer Bear

Overcoming Violence in the Name of Religion (Christianity and Islam)

Hermann Häring

'There is no compulsion in religion' (Qur'an II, 256)

No Christian, nor Muslim either, should still dispute the fact that wherever Christianity and Islam have gained power and respect they have been accompanied by a history of violence. They have not only legitimated and tacitly allowed violence, but have also provoked and practised it, encouraging fantasies of violence even though they know better. That tells against the claim of Christianity and Islam to offer salvation. However, no critic of Christianity or Islam should dispute the fact that the emancipation of Western culture from religious domination has not stemmed the practice of violence but rather intensified it, finally leading to monstrous eruptions of violence. The worst and most abhorrent crimes of our century were committed in the names of anti-religious ideologies, National Socialism and Stalinism.

However, the relationship between religion and violence is quite diffuse, and there is always another side which forms the background to their vague proximity: the almost universal humanizing and healing function of religion. Religions provide orientation, comfort and an ethic of empathy. That can be traced today right into the misery of any megalopolis: networks of solidarity, mutual help and resistance keep appearing afresh, often as a matter of course. Without this everyday stemming of violence Christianity and Islam, too, would not have conquered cultures and survived for centuries.

Nevertheless they have a weak point. They tend to violence as soon as their identity is threatened. Their own dissidents are the first to suffer a continual threat of exclusion, oppression and violent measures. Where a society no longer allows physical violence, the mechanisms are refined and transformed into psychological and social repression. Conversely, it can be taken to be a basic rule that non-violent resolutions of external conflicts can probably succeed only if it is possible to resolve internal conflicts in a non-violent way. Therefore every religion has to be asked, 'How do you deal with your dissidents, i.e. with those who diverge at a central point from the common teaching and practice of faith?' Is it possible to excommunicate dissidents, to exclude them from the community of faith and even hand them over to Satan (I Cor. 5.5)? Or is it not finally time to see to it that the resolutions of conflicts are non-violent?

I. The legacy of violence

Before I go into this, some open and self-critical comments are called for. Otherwise the answer would be superficial and not go beyond the bounds of a general liberal impulse. It must be evident that from the beginning Christianity and Islam have offered manifest examples: their capacity to act called for clear conditions. Two examples from the letters of Paul may suffice. The first shows how convinced Paul was of his own truth: 'If any one is preaching to you a gospel contrary to that which we preached to you, let him be accursed' (Gal. 1.8). The second shows that such curses were connected with the deepest convictions of faith: 'If anyone has no love for the Lord, let him be accursed. Our Lord, come.'[1] Excommunications were then the order of the day. Priscillian was the first Christian 'heretic', and he paid for his dissent in 385 with his death. What was still generally condemned at that time met with similarly general approval a century later. Islam zealously emulated Christianity on this point. Here, too, true faith was to remain unsullied. The mystic Al Hallaj, who was accused of pantheism, was executed in 922 for heresy and political crimes. The great theologian and philosopher Averroes was put in the stocks at the 'Door of Grace' of the mosque in Cordoba in 1195 for heresy and then banished to the East for showing hostility to religion in his writings. But the Christian and Muslim history of the persecution of heretics need not be repeated here. It is a background which warns us to be realistic. So some questions should be enough.

1. Historical

The reactions against dissidents become harsher, the more the reputation, influence and unity of the faith community are at stake. At the latest in the Christian Middle Ages, heresy was understood as a public crime and punished with all the harshness of the law, including the sword and the stake. A small community will react with internal discussions, perhaps harsh ones. There is a good reason why compulsion and violence play a lesser role among the Shiites than they do among the Sunnis, whose rulers became the heads of Muslim kingdoms. There is also good reason why the Protestant churches, which experienced intolerance and exclusion themselves, deal more cautiously with their dissidents than the Catholic Church. But even this did not exclude harsher measures when the social order was an issue. Thus as early as 1553 Servetus was condemned to death and burned at Calvin's instigation. So historical experience shows that increasing social influence leads to increasing violence. Does that mean that Christianity and Islam should renounce any influence on society?

2. Political

It seems that in the long run a systematic and legally controlled fight against heresy is crowned with success. There were regular debates on questions of faith in the early church, carried on with theological skill. The legal institution of the Inquisition developed in Christian Europe, like the legal institution of the Mihna in the Baghdad Caliphate in the ninth century. In both religions, a differentiated way of suppressing heresy was practised; heresies were determined and discussed, and then the heretics were called on to recant. It is hard to compare concrete practices, because a central control of faith never developed in Islam; it remained dependent on the power and religious zeal of individual rulers and dynasties. The growing centralism of the Roman church increased its effectiveness and cruelty. From 1252 Rome allowed torture in interrogations. This smoothed the way for cruelty: the state authorities were given the task of burning condemned heretics. In 1542 the Inquisition was formed as the central Roman institution, and its successor still exists today under the title 'Congregation of Faith' (though in changed circumstances). In modern times the Catholic Church has developed extremely rigid and intolerant rules; these may no longer affect the physical integrity of victims, but they do affect their psychological integrity. One need think only of Teilhard de Chardin, who was banished to China and died a lonely death in New York in 1955. It may be unpleasant, but it is true: the Catholic Church had success, as it understood success, with this unyielding practice. For centuries it could present itself as a stronghold of unity. By contrast the Reformation churches and the later churches of the eighteenth and nineteenth centuries had no success, presenting themselves as places of constant disunity and division. Are not communities of faith called on to show such unity if they are to survive?

3. Sociological

In the course of the centuries the two religions have radiated a tremendous amount of intolerance and self-justification, and practised mental and physical violence. Here ideological and power-political interests may always have been a factor. But why have believers not defended themselves against the doings of theologians and religious leaders? The reason for this may be that the real dissidents were not superficial disturbers of the peace but were often ahead of their time, arousing deep anxieties and causing unrest to soul and spirit. It was felt that they were critics of a power and order on which the faith depended. From the perspective of social psychology, harsh reactions against religious dissidents were therefore not a sign of a narrow-minded self-defence, but were meant as support to those who did not want to leave their protected sphere. Only where resistance movements developed out of individual dissidents did the representatives of religion find themselves in a crisis situation of argumentation and acceptance. Do not the majority of believers expect protection from unnecessary disruption?

4. Theological

In dealing with dissidents, Christianity and Islam certainly also tend towards compulsion and violence, because they are prophetic religions. The prophetic religions explain the world and create certainty, enthusiasm and the courage to change the world and society. So Christians and Muslims uncompromisingly seek God's will, and are convinced that in their actions they are acting in accordance with God's will. Plans to shape the world appear as the utopia of the kingdom of God. Christians and Muslims experience God's word and truth so directly that they believe that anyone of good will must understand them. According to Paul, the unbeliever will come in, listen, fall on his knees and exclaim, 'God is indeed among you' (I Cor. 14.24). Perhaps the odd word may be misunderstood, but it would be unforgivable to close one's heart to the truth: 'Whoever says a word against the Son of Man will be forgiven; but whoever speaks against the Holy Spirit will not be forgiven, either in this age or in the age to come' (Matt. 12.32). The same thing can be demonstrated in the history of the foundation of Islam, the crisis of which is paradigmatically recorded in Muhammad's *hijra* to Medina and the abiding claim to the Ka'ba in Mecca. Muhammad appeals to Abraham and thus undermines the claims of the Jews (with Moses) and the Christians (with Jesus as prophet). Despite the original and lasting tolerance towards Jews and Christians (the 'people of the book'), a final alternative presents itself which can no longer be overcome by human beings. An indispensable claim arises out of the inclusion of Jews and Christians: 'If they accept your faith, they shall be rightly guided; if they reject it, they shall surely be in schism. Against them God is your all-sufficient defender' (Surah 2.135–8). Does not an unbridgable opposition arise here, as soon as others think that they can reject a conviction recognized as God's truth?'

II. The claim of modernity

Thus at this point problems arise, for intrinsically religious and theological reasons, which cannot be resolved by any modern liberalism. The contradictions in our society go deeper than the call for tolerance.

Convictions of faith always appear as a simple option: they cannot be thought of or held without exclusion and otherness. In that case there is only the alternative 'Satan or God?', which seems to break through all liberalism. In the New Testament we read, 'Satan has demanded to have you to sift you like wheat' (Luke 22.31). The Qur'an says: 'God is the Patron of the faithful. He leads them from darkness to the light. As for the unbelievers, their patrons are false gods, who led them from light to darkness. They are the heirs of Hell and shall abide in it for ever.'[2] In times of crisis this clarificatory rule is simplified even further. The spirit, theologically speaking, is turned into the letter. Critics are excluded out of hand or denounced; the protection of the truth is identified with institutional interests. The danger of any enthusiasm is then fanaticism and finally the annihilation of the dissidents. Arguments are instrumentalized; everything is combined in the intoxication of a perverted and merciless religious feeling. The doors are then opened to the horror of public execution and the triumph of the executioner, the restless intoxication of torture,[3] the cynicism of the acute zealot and the hypocrisy of those who think that they are always right before God and the world.

1. Democratic practice

Against this background a historical experience of the nineteenth and twentieth centuries becomes especially significant. A fundamental aim of society is to overcome violence at every level, to control long-term potential for violence, to disarm it or to transform it into productive solutions. This aim is also imposed on religions in particular. Now I do not want here to trace the manifestly religious roots of this modern thought, which can be combined with concepts like the dignity and freedom of the person.[4] Rather, I want to use this idea heuristically and raise the question: what possibilities for settling violence in connection with dissidents can be found in the traditions of Christianity and Islam?

Let us go back, as far as is historically possible, to the period of origins, when the original rules were perhaps still manifest. Christians know the rules for the community in the Gospel of Matthew: 'If you are offering your gift at the altar, and there remember that your brother has something against you, leave your gift there before the altar and go; first be reconciled to your brother, and then come and offer your gift.'[5] This rule is so vivid and uncompromising because the offering (the blood that has not run) is surely useless after the reconciliation. So forget sacrificial rituals as long as you have anything against a brother or sister. Something else is even more important here, since it stems from the possibility of resolving all conflicts in a conversation regulated by the institution. In cases of conflict there must first be confidential conversation and then a conversation before witnesses. Then the community is brought in. Only if this conversation has no success is the accused treated 'as a pagan or a tax collector' (Matt. 18.15–17). There is no disputing the fact that this way of running the Christian community did not last very long. The more a hierarchy came under the pressure of difficult doctrinal discussions and growing social responsibility, the more clearly hierarchical governments took responsibility for laying down doctrinal rules.

Now as is well known, the Qur'an indefatigably inculcates the readiness of the All-Merciful to forgive, and this also involves the readiness to forgive third parties and one another. 'Muhammad is God's Messenger. Those who follow him are ruthless to the unbelievers but merciful to one another' (Sura 48,29). But are there no specific rules? Mohammed Arkoun points to Sura 42, which plays a great role in the Muslim discussion. Evidently it has preserved recollections from the early period of Medina under the title 'Counsel' (al Shura). It is about those 'who obey their Lord, attend to their prayers, and conduct their affairs by mutual consent; who bestow in alms a part of what We have given them' (42,38). So discussion in the community (*umma*) is one of the basic demands of the early period. Sura 3,159 is also important; this requires of the Prophet himself towards believers, 'Pardon them, and implore God to forgive them. Take counsel with them in the conduct of affairs.' With increasing emphasis this reminiscence is interpreted as a reference to an early democratic practice coupled with pardon and prayer for forgiveness. This was the time when Muhammad surrounded himself with ten leading men from various clans.

2. Strengthening authority

However (as in Christianity), this democratic line does not exclude a first line of legitimation, from God through the founder to the present authority. Now the *umma* is no longer understood as the community which 'can deceive neither itself nor others', but is put under the authority of the Prophet: 'Believers, obey God and obey the Messenger and those in authority among you. Should you disagree about anything, refer it to God and the Messenger, if you truly believe in God and the Last Day. This will in the end be better and more just' (4,59). The first four caliphs then understand themselves as 'followers of God's Messenger' in this sense, and claim his indirect authority. Only after the great split between Sunnis and Shiites did an autocratic ruling institution come into being in which the

Umayyads and subsequent dynasties then understand themselves –
directly and in an undisguised way – as representatives of God on earth
(how similar the developments are!). The Shiite group reacted to this
sensitively. It is their imams who are given an absolute teaching authority,
who are often described in the literature as having moral and theological
infallibility.[6] So are they the representatives of the Catholic line in Islam?

3. Limits of authority

The situation is more complex. It cannot be sweepingly maintained that
Islam knows only a hierarchical system. Certainly, 'From the time of the
Umayyads, the transfer of the charismatic authority of the prophet to the
sacralized power of the caliphs, the emirs and the sultans became the
political and cultural practice of the so-called Muslim societies.'[7] But there
is also the charismatic authority of mystical orders and there is the spiritual
power of the imams, who were increasingly clearly distinguished from the
Sunni claims to hierocratic power. The brokenness of the last authority
becomes particularly clear in the conviction that the Twelfth Imam lives in
secret and his return must be awaited. One day he will return, break the
rule of the tyrants and establish a kingdom of justice. Granted, qualified
Shiite theologians are given the right of the *fatwa* (an infallible legal
pronouncement), but this is simply the arbitration of an individual and can
be relativized by other decisions. So in Shiite Islam there is a model in
which the fragility of the teaching office emerges. Violence is really not
possible as its consequence. This conception in particular was misused by
Khomeini in the Iranian revolution. He abruptly anticipated the final
authority of the Twelfth Imam and established a regime of the worst
possible violence in the name of truth.[8]

There is a problem here for Islam which also emerges in the Christian
tradition. It has two consequences:
– The question of violence cannot be resolved until it becomes the focus of
reflection. So we must recognize that violence cannot be a solution as long
as God is a God of mercy and love.
– The question of violence is always rife in prophetic religions. So
Christians and Muslims are well advised to take seriously modern
experiences of controlling and overcoming violence.

As world religions, Christianity and Islam embarked upon a new phase
of their existence in the nineteenth century. New cultural, social and
political environments also led to a reorientation inwards. Defensive
reactions (from anti-modernism to new authoritarian and fundamentalist
trends) have not got us any further. Meanwhile it has become clear at many
points of Christian and Muslim culture that compulsion or violence,
whether understood physically or psychologically, are no longer convinc-

ing ways of giving God's will its due. There is need for a revitalization of communication, a democratic attitude and an appropriate differentiation of functions. Against this background the following rules can apply in dealing with dissidents.

III. Resolving conflicts

1. *Conversation with the person concerned*

There are conflicts and pseudo-conflicts. The main goal for any community is the preservation of freedom, justice and peace. All real conflicts about which the community has to decide can be related to one of these three dimensions. Now conflicts are not objective, and therefore objectifiable, processes but processes of communication in which the parties in the conflict and their public are always already involved. So it would be wrong either to suppress conflicts or to project them. Both these things happen in religious communities. The suppression of conflicts (mostly to protect the privileged) poisons the atmosphere and often prevents the discussion of life-threatening problems. The projection of conflicts (usually to the disadvantage of the person concerned) creates mistrust and develops a dynamic of its own, ultimately resulting in conflicts which cannot be resolved.

So a settlement of the conflict which does justice to the truth and protects the person accused must first answer the question: to what degree and to what extent is there a conflict? Is the problem merely incidental, a misunderstanding or a problem in communication? Are there uncompromising polarizations or a conflict that can be resolved at a substantive level with professional help? Is the conflict simply disturbing the community, or are central religious positions involved? To clarify these questions it is natural and advisable (and required by both Bible and Qur'an) for those involved to be given a personal hearing and to discuss together – prior to more formal steps to settle the conflict.

2. *Clear rules of procedure*

This point is worth mentioning because it brings out a problem of religious organizations. Roman legal practice has certainly bound itself to usable rules, but often enough it uses them against the spirit of brotherhood and sisterhood. This can be demonstrated in detail from the case of Hans Küng, which is particularly well documented.[9] Numerous other theologians have been the victim of quite obscure procedures which could not be followed through by investigations. New humiliating punishments have been devised, e.g. long-term 'penitential silence' (as in the case of Leonardo Boff) or the assertion that a theologian has excommunicated himself by his statements (as in the case of Tissa Balasuriya). Finally, an attitude is constantly shown which makes the curia appear the mistress of proceedings while refusing the accused any ultimate respect. Cases of the blatant use of violence from the Islamic sphere are sufficiently well known (Salman Rushdie, Abu Zaid). It is beyond dispute that such a procedure flagrantly goes against the spirit of both the Bible and the Qur'an.

Here three spans are needed, to bridge universality and context, origin and present, individuality and public. They can show us whether and how compulsion can be prevented and dissent taken seriously as such.

3. Mediation between universality and context

Christians and Muslims have sufficient experience of mediation between universality and context. Though the Qur'an is one, the message of Islam has been adapted to the most different Islamic worlds from Indonesia to Algeria. Sunnis, Shiites and other groups have existed side by side for centuries. The Christian world knows many denominations; each of them has its own legal system and resolves its conflicts in its own way. At a universal Christian level, i.e. at the level of the World Council of Churches, only conversations and mutual agreement can produce good results. Since the Second Vatican Council the Catholic Church has increasingly emphatically discovered its local multiplicity and at the same time has remained a world church. We have learned from Third World theologians that at the end of our century resolutions of conflicts are possible only when cultures, genders, and social and political conditions are taken seriously; new, concrete truth comes into being where dissidents are not suppressed but taken seriously.

4. Translation from origin to present

Modernity is proving to have an unprecedented historical consciousness. Since the nineteenth century, Christianity and Islam have perceived the changes, and for a long time have reacted in a split way, i.e. with both dialogue and rejection. In Christianity the development has been expressed in a long and painful process of theological reflection. We know how – more resolutely than in static times – we have to remember that on the one hand we are co-authors in our present reading of scripture. Here a fundamentalist recourse to scripture is not a helpful solution. Therefore the contribution of everyone involved, along with experts, is needed in the resolution of conflicts within religions. The experts are not there to replace the tradition by secular scholarship, but to help to interpret it more appropriately.

Christian theologians are fond of pointing out that they are ahead of their Muslim colleagues in freedom and in the non-violent discussion of interpretation of their scriptures. But often we overestimate our own practice and underestimate the practice of Islam. In the Christian churches new, contextual, feminist, culturally focussed interpretations are still often marginalized. At the same time the Qur'an has always been accessible to time-conditioned interpretations. One need think only of the large-scale acceptance of Greek philosophy and other sciences in the Middle Ages and the rich range of scholarly methods which Christians have learned from Islam. Finally, we usually do not perceive that Muslim scholars have already long been involved in a committed and highly sophisticated discussion of the scholarly understanding of the Qur'an, which is concerned for its meaning today.

> In Muslim lands today there are authorized voices, understandings of renewal, but they are intimidated or silenced by the activists who are 'making history'. It is of vital interest for the few scholars and thinkers who are capable of it to stimulate reflection, and emerge from their self-imposed or compulsory reserve: not to consolidate their triumphalist discourse and not to share the fruits of the people's battle with the 'militants', but to implement the rights of the free and questioning spirit, a concrete and indispensable authority.[10]

5. Respect for individuality and openness

So far little attention has been paid to this. Already in the framework of the Catholic definition of infallibility in the 1970s, it was often pointed out that in the nineteenth century a third force was established alongside magisterium and theology: public opinion. This force has often either markedly alienated or intensified discussions within religions. It often produces new forms of violence: incomplete information or misinformation, instigation and manipulation; the misuse of religious knowledge and religious experience for power-political or financial ends. The use of the media by church authorities or dissidents often creates a tendency towards violence. Beyond question the media today are falsifying the situation of Islam and its conflicts. Islam has been made a band of modern fanatics and this has led to violence in the circles of the dissidents. Here I do not approve of a single murder, a single death sentence, a single hate-filled cry. But it has to be said that such publicity makes it almost impossible to break through the vicious circle into which some Islamic countries and an appeal to their religion have been driven.

Conclusion

Those who want to overcome violence credibly must overcome its legitimation, whether manifest or concealed, in their own communities. Dealing with one's own dissidents is the test case here. Christians and Muslims have not done well in this test in the past. That makes the chances for the future all the better, the less Christianity and Islam succumb to the seduction of worldly power. The history of both religions in dealing with dissidents shows amazing parallels. In both, the institutional power of the doctrinal definition has been dominant. But it has also become clear to both that renewal and the non-violent resolution of conflicts is possible only through an authentic return to their own sources. Moreover in both religions it is increasingly being said that violence cannot be a means of resolving internal problems. How could that be in religions which confess an all-merciful, loving God?[11] Is the overcoming of violence, of compulsion, of over-hasty excommunication, of all the mechanisms of unjust exclusion, possible in dealing with dissidents? This will always remain difficult. But it will be all the more successful if the religions, their communities and representatives keep to the rules given above.

Translated by John Bowden

Notes

1. I Cor. 16.22. This problem has never been worked out properly in the context of religious law, see E. Käsemann, 'Sentences of Holy Law in the New Testament', in *New Testament Questions of Today*, London and Philadelphia 1969, 66–81.

2. Surah 2,257. For this reason rules were already made in the early church which allowed no discussions. Anyone who speaks with charismatic authority, i.e. anyone who speaks credibly in the name of the Spirit, has a claim to be obeyed: 'In the name of the Lord Jesus, when you are assembled, and my spirit is present, you are to deliver this man to Satan' (I Cor. 5.4f.). This also seems to apply to the authority of the apostle. In the Qur'an we read: 'The infidels fight for the devil. Fight then against the friends of Satan' (Surah 4,76).

3. W. Sofsky, *Traktat über die Gewalt*, Frankfurt 1996, shows how these manifestations of cruelty develop a terrible dynamic of their own.

4. There is no question that the concept of the dignity and freedom of the person does not just rest on the biblical or Christian image of human beings. It also takes up Muslim tradition, which is not necessarily close to that of Christianity. The Muslim scholar Hasan Hanafi (who gained his doctorate at the Sorbonne in 1966), writes: 'Despite the weight given to the emphasis on Muslim identity, the rejection of any dissolution of Muslim identity and the criticism of Westernism, it has to be noted that the rejection of everything Western (parliamentary institutions, representation, democratic tendencies, liberal movements) makes the Muslim revolution a reaction rather than an action. It is a transition from colonialism to hostility to everything

Western. Nevertheless rationalism, secularization, science, democracy, naturalism, humanism, progressivism are all Muslim tendencies on which the world has constantly drawn: in the Middle Ages, the periods of the Reformation and the Renaissance, and in modern times. So it is possible to take part in the revolution of reason in the West or in the clergy revolution in Latin America' (quoted in Mohammed Arkoun, *Pour une critique de la raison islamique*, Paris 1984, 182).

5. Matt. 5.23. Cf. also Matt. 18.22 (one is to forgive 'not seven times but seventy times seven') and Matt. 7.5 ('First take the log out of your own eye, and then you will see clearly to take the speck out of your brother's eye').

6. W. Ende et al. (ed.), *Der Islam in der Gegenwart*, Munich 1984.

7. Arkoun, *Pour une critique* (n. 4), 174.

8. According to Khomeini, the power of the Mahdi was now given representatively to the most qualified legal expert (himself) because the *shariah* had been completely abrogated; but this is not allowed (Surah 4.60).

9. W. Jens (ed.), *Um nichts als die Wahrheit. Deutsche Bischofskonferenz contra Hans Küng. Eine Dokumentation*, Munich 1978; N. Greinacher and H. Haag, *Der Fall Küng. Eine Dokumentation*, Munich 1980.

10. Arkoun, *Pour une critique* (n. 4), 185. However, since I do not know Arabic, I concede that I can mention only a few names: Zaki Naguib Nahmud, Tarif Khalidi, Abdallah Laroui, Mohammed Arkoun, Tariq al-Bishri (L. Binder, *Islamic Liberation. A Critique of Development Ideologies*, Chicago 1988).

11. 'A return to the Qur'an is needed to overcome the divisions and divergences which have constantly split the Umma in the past. It contains all the clear and comprehensive statements which have to be implemented by an Islamic government' (Arkoun, *Pour une critique* [n. 4], 184).

III · Analyses and Conclusions

Working Hard to Overcome Violence in the Name of Religion

Hermann Häring

Between the production and the overcoming of violence

The affinity between violence and religion is manifest, and attested by countless facts from history and the present. The sociology and psychology of religion have produced detailed investigations. None of the great religions can be acquitted of the charge of violence. However, we Christians are in a danger of falling from one cliché into another. In times of cultural certainty and continuity we saw the Christian religion one-sidedly as a religion of reconciliation, peace, love of one's neighbour and one's enemy. The Sermon on the Mount with its summons to non-violence was thought to be unique and Christianity therefore to be the climax and consummation of all religion. In recent decades the mood has changed. We have come to recognize our potential for violence. With shame we recall the times of the crusades and colonialism, when Christians fell in love with power and spiritual domination; we remember our affinity to antisemitism and Fascist regimes, and finally Auschwitz, which still cannot be coped with in any theological categories. The mechanisms of exclusion and extermination worked perfectly. Doubts have gnawed away in particular at the hearts of convinced Christians: is not Christianity deeply a religion of violence and incapable of overcoming it?

In any criticism of religion this question can be rapidly expanded. Does not the charge apply to all religions, e.g. for Islam, as can be demonstrated today anywhere? Have we not experienced the war in the Balkans between Catholics, Orthodox and Muslims; the violent clashes in northern India with the Sikhs; the religiously motivated disturbances in Timor? Has there not been a religious war in Ireland for decades now? Violence seems to lead to tremendous explosions where religion becomes the motive for political action.

The view that religion necessarily leads to violence is as one-sided as the earlier supposition that Christianity or any other world religions necessarily led to peace. The interconnections are complicated; that is already evident from the fact that religion only leads to violence when it is associated with other factors. These can be national interests or political oppression; there are moments of social uncertainty or cultural upheaval. Religions can be misused, and misdirected from outside or inside. In that case they fuel outbreaks of violence. But the eras of violence in the world religions have always been opposed, and have led to ways of overcoming violence. In the history of Christianity one could think of the objections to slavery and the subjection of the Indios, the objections to the witch craze and the persecution of the Jews. One might think of the countless civil rights movements against local wars and terrorist regimes, against military rearmament and social injustice, against the exclusion of those who hold different religious views.

So for our own encouragement and orientation it is important for us also to be aware of the constant opposition movements and all the many individuals who have often worked in the name of their religion to overcome social, political or religious violence. They have often been quite successful. That they have never been completely successful is not surprising, given the situation of human beings and the world. We human beings are prone to violence and our histories are stamped by experiences of violence. It is for the religions to oppose this violence, to assimilate it and overcome it productively. That happens every day and in all religions. However, as a rule little is known of those groups which assimilate and overcome violence. This article is divided into three parts. First it will discuss the criticism of violence in all religions. Then it will mention some instances of criticism of violence in the present. Finally reference will be made to specific problems in the present criticism of violence: how can we really overcome violence?

I. Criticism of violence in all religions

1. Eastern religions

All the great religions are critical about the use of violence and have strong movements which express this criticism. One thinks of Taoism and above all of Confucianism which (like all the other world religions) knows the Golden Rule: 'What you would not want to be done to you, do not do to others.' That is not yet a summons to unconditional non-violence, but a call for the overcoming of violence.[1] Then there is Brahmanism and, after it, Buddhism. Brahmanism describes, say in the Rig Veda, the nucleus of all wrong human behaviour as *himsa* (= 'violence'). So for Brahmanism renunciation of violence is the decisive demand. It forms the nucleus of good and healthy modes of behaviour which overcome disaster. Thus the concept of *ahimsa* ('non-violence') becomes a central concept of Brahmanist ethics. *Ahimsa* does not seek to harm or to violate anything. All life is caught up in the great cycle of *karma*, and thus must be treated with great respect; it may not be disturbed, far less destroyed from outside. Whereas the foundation of *ahimsa* (from the perspective of a Western ethic orientated on the well-being of men and women) may not perhaps attain the uncompromising quality and concentration of Christian love of neighbour, its effect is universal and much more understandable, since it puts the integrity of life and the world at the centre of action without any qualification. We may take it as certain that Gandhi, who has strongly shaped the present-day understanding of *ahimsa* inspired by the Jainism of his youth, drew heavily on this impetus.[2]

Buddha's instruction that no suffering is to be caused to others is very much in line with this basic attitude. The abolition of evil is the goal of the Eightfold Path. Buddha, like a doctor, is concerned with practice and healing, not with a doctrine or religious theory. Because of this practical goal he warns against clinging to doctrines of religious salvation, even though these are his own views. He calls for tolerance and issues an unconditional prohibition against killing life. Kindness, sympathy, the sharing of joy and serenity are for him the four central actions which are to permeate all behaviour.[3] Against the background of such a spirituality it is not surprising that the mentality of Christianity is felt to be aggressive, as we shall see later in more detail.

2. Islam

It should not be forgotten that Islam, too, has a strong and old stream of non-violence. This may seem surprising, and the situation is certainly more difficult to survey than in Hinduism and Buddhism. Despite the often conciliatory tone to be found in the Qur'an, everything in Islam seems to be attuned to conquest and fighting. Like the other monotheistic religions, Islam is concerned with the active shaping of a just world. In contrast to Buddhism, the missionary goals of conversation and the dissemination of the faith are legitimate and even called for under certain conditions. The conception of a common life shaped in accordance with the Qur'an and the *shariah* seems virtually to require at least violence regulated by the state and the resolute implementation of Allah's will. Nevertheless, we should not forget that Islam too arose for different motives. In Medina the dismantling and overcoming of violence are already the goal in building up a just community. So as in any Western social ethic with a Christian foundation, pressure is exerted (by the state) to prevent violence. And we should not forget that Allah, the One God and Creator of the World, is already consistently called ar-Rahman, the 'all-merciful' or 'One who has Mercy', in the Qur'an. Although this God requires submission, he is not a despot, and although Islam knows no incarnation of God or divine brotherhood, Allah is at all events a good God: 'God's mercifulness contains a good deal of the fatherliness which we look upon as typically Christian.'[4] So at the heart of Muslim faith we find trust and gratitude; this is already expressed by the term *islam*, which is to be translated as devotion or surrender. Thus 'unbelief' means the ingratitude of the creature towards the one to whom it owes everything, namely goodness, mercy, life and salvation.

It is therefore not suprising that particularly in Islam a mysticism of tremendous intensity, so-called Sufism, has developed. Granted, this happened in opposition to the official and always predominant doctrinal tradition, but Sufism has shaped the history of Islam more clearly than Christian mysticism has shaped Christianity.[5] Islam has not developed any mysticism which withdraws from the world or sinks into the all or Nirvana, like that in the East. It has developed its personal picture of God in accordance with a mysticism of pure encounter. The Muslim mysticism of the encounter of God is not 'diverted' christologically, as often happens in Christianity. Its experience is quite direct: an almost blazing encounter with God, in which the I is completely dissolved, so that here the notion of non-violence gains ground for spiritual reasons. But does not such a mysticism lead away from the ideal of shaping the world, so that Sufism condemns itself to ineffectiveness, and withdraws from situations of violence instead of overcoming them?

All experts in Islam point out that the mystic tendencies of Islam were not and are an individual matter. Sufism was always centred in religious communities, which shaped the consciousness and attitudes of Muslim believers and kept opening their minds to notions of friendliness, mercy and non-violence. Time and again these communities have been contested by 'orthodox' tendencies orientated on doctrine, nationalistic and prepared to use violence. The reason is understandable: what is central here is not the fight to defend Islam, but immersion in God's mercy, which seeks its due place in this world. Thus the principle of loving one's enemy is not yet formulated as the extreme boundary statement, though a spirituality of love of fellow human beings and a readiness for reconciliation puts down deep roots.

3. Interim comment

However, the question is whether and how these experiences of surrender, friendliness and non-violence can become established in a monotheistic prophetic religion (to anticipate the argument, that also applies to the biblical criticism of violence). Two factors should be noted which, in contrast to Hinduism, prevent non-violence from being taken for granted at the deepest level. The first factor is the concentration of the monotheistic religions on human salvation, the anthropocentricity of their thought. Salvation is their prime concern: the world and non-human life are made to serve this purpose. Therefore violence against the world and life is allowed more readily than in the Eastern religions. The world and life are subordinated, sometimes even instrumentalized, for the sake of human beings. The second factor is the passion for fulfilling God's will which these 'prophetic' religions have developed. The world is to be transformed and justice is to be established. Can we or must we not use violence in some circumstances as a means to higher ends?

Now of course this indicates that violence is not one entity among others, nor is it a phenomenon that can be isolated in human action. For example, sexuality shows how easy it is to move from expressions of love to violent domination. Violence, compulsion and oppression occur throughout life and are regarded by many as an indispensable element in human life. Anyone who wants to abolish violence, overcome conditions of violence and change the world, in other words anyone who wants to create a just society, will continually feel called to exert compulsion and will have to exercise violence, at least in situations of self-defence. So even an ordered society must keep dealing with violence. According to the Western understanding of the democratic state, states rightly claim a monopoly of violence regulated by law. So in individual and social life it is not simply a matter of saying yes or no to violence. Often we have to use violence to prevent even worse violence, to remove violence with calculated counter-violence, or to use violence against animals and things on behalf of human beings. It is therefore the task of a good Jewish, Christian or Muslim policy to make appropriate decisions, but ones which can have some effect.[6] I shall not be going into this further here. I simply want to make clear why, particularly in prophetic religions, the ideal of non-violence is constantly threatened and endangered for a good end. It is a matter of defining statements and almost utopian goals. So prophetic religions have to cope with a tremendous intrinsic tension. Precisely for that reason there are often such terrible explosions in religions which are critical of violence.

4. The biblical tradition

Only when this has been said should we remember how intensively the biblical tradition grapples with the problem of violence. It finds the question of violence a specific problem. The first eleven chapters of Genesis understand the history of humankind as a history of the spread of violence; only God can put a stop to it, and then only by taking radical steps. At the same time this history is the basis of biblical, i.e. primarily Jewish, realism, which has experienced it time and again and is convinced that the history of humankind has always been shaped by violence and will always be dogged by it. By contrast, God always forgives, and God does not give up his promises. God shows himself as love (Hos. 11.8) and offers the prospect of access to his final peace. Swords will be beaten into ploughshares (Isa. 32.4). However, this goal of a non-violent future raises the question: can violence still be a means to this end, or is not suffering better than violence? Is it not better to transcend this utopia of salvation in the form of the suffering servant (Isa. 52.13–ch.53) than in the form of the powerful royal champion of God's triumph? The utopia of healing suffering, a limiting statement of supreme religious intensity, has found an inalienable place in the Jewish tradition. The unique significance of Jesus, who has gone down in the history of religions as the Crucified One, is then grounded in this tradition. Later, time and again the significance of Jesus is summed up in the suffering as a focal point: the focus of his message is expressed in the Sermon on the Mount as the summons to unconditional non-violence and love of enemy.[7] The Sermon on the Mount and the Cross interpret each other.

But in the Christian tradition, too, the ideal of non-violence is countered by a use of violence which has a foundation in everyday religion. The story of Jesus' passion is often misused as a legitimation of later suffering. At the same time the tremendous political, technical and economic power which has accrued to the Christian churches has made the temptation to the everyday use of violence, a world-wide sense of superiority and a spiritual and material imperialism irresistible. So the question remains whether the religions can still realize their call to overcome violence at all, particularly when they are successful as institutions.

II. Examples of the religious criticism of violence today

1. *Minorities*

Violence can be contained, prevented or overcome in a great many ways. It cannot be finally exterminated. All religious criticism of violence must begin by being realistic about this. The work begins afresh every day. The Christian tradition has a rich history of groups which have specifically committed themselves to the criticism of violence and to non-violence. Until the fourth century, the waging of war and Christian faith were thought incompatible; for 'in God there is no violence'.[8] After that the critics were in a minority. The classical critics of violence in modern times, which refer to the Sermon on the Mount, are the pacifist churches: the Mennonites (sixteenth century), the Brotherhood movement (seventeenth century) and the Quakers (eighteenth century). They have subscribed to non-violence in principle and therefore most of the time have been forced to engage in civil disobedience. Because of their refusal to swear oaths and serve in the army, as a rule they have suffered political persecution. But they have been a thorn in the flesh of the great churches, since they have good biblical arguments on their side.

So it can only surprise us how little following these Christian critics of violence found up to the time of the Second World War. In Germany for example, the conscientious objectors of the Second World War still have not been rehabilitated, even when the ethical or religious motives of their action at that time are manifest. Meanwhile progress is to be noted. In the modern democracies the social and political significance of dissidents has gradually been recognized, at least in recent decades. However, the term has lost its original religious significance.[9] It denotes all those who are committed to the preservation of human rights contrary to the official policy of a country. The dissident groups in Russia sought publicity with Alexander Solzhenitzyn as one of the great spokesmen with religious motivation. The dissident movement in the former Czech Soviet Republic should also be mentioned. It, too, had some religious motivation, though the arguments of the spokesman who is best known today, Vaclav Havel, were secular and humanist. The dissident movements which (with strong Christian motivation) at the end of the 1960s pressed for an end to the Vietnam War (1936–1975) and raised questions about racism and militarism were also of world-wide significance. This was the time when all over the world such movements became established for the overcoming of colonialism, imperialism and dictatorship. In all of them the motivation included a strong religious element. However, those who have a strong religious motivation also argue in political or anthropological terms, or on the basis of human rights, in order to achieve a wide consensus. The fact that they have been and remain minorities does not mean that they have not had some success in bringing about political change and shaping of consciences.

2. Hinduism and Buddhism

It is difficult to locate clearly the countless groups or movements which are critical of violence and society, to describe their motives or to assess their political and religious significance. The transitions from protest on specific issues to far-reaching political dissent are as blurred as the scale of motives and reasons. Protest is often formulated in purely human and political terms, or in terms of human rights, but equally often there are strong religious motives behind it.[10] However, it would be perverse to limit the existence of protest groups and movements to Christian culture. There are politically effective movements which are critical of violence in all the world religions. The Muslim journalist Hagen Berndt points out that today people are working intensively towards non-violence in every religious culture, supported by the spiritual sources of their religion.[11] He mentions the Burmese opposition politician and Nobel Peace prize-winner Aung San Suu Kyi, who indefatigably organizes the non-violent resistance to the military regime in her country, motivated by Buddhism. He mentions the Vietnamese Zen monk Thich Nhat Hanh, who in 1964 founded the School of Youth for Social Service in Saigon, and from 1966 has lived in exile in France; at that time he was supported by Thomas Merton. Together with Sulak Sivaraksa (Alternative Peace Price, 1995), Thich Nhat Hanh works in the latter's International Network of Engaged Buddhists (INEB), with settlements in twenty-six countries. And there is the monk Omalpe Sobhia Thero, head of a Buddhist temple in Sri Lanka, who attacks the image of a Buddhism sunk in inwardness and is clearly showing the Buddhist monasteries that they have a task of criticizing society. Finally, Berndt mentions the aged monk Maha Ghosananda, who since 1979 has sought to create trust in a peaceful future by annual marches through battered Cambodia. He issues a call to leave the temples and enter the temples of human experience with their tremendous suffering.

3. Islam

Berndt also gives impressive examples from Islam, where especially the mystical tradition over the centuries has created many forms of non-violent approach to conflicts. Their concern is reconciliation and the preservation of social relationships. The movement of the Khudai Khidmatgar ('servants of God') in north-west India is widely known. Abdul Ghaffar Khan founded it and obligated its members to recognize the principle of non-violence, to be committed to the well-being of all creatures and the freedom of the oppressed, and to refuse all military service.

For twenty years non-violent activists have been working in southern Thailand in the Muslim-inspired Civil Rights Protection Centre. They fight against violations of human rights and expressly set God's commandment against the state violence of their land; here they enjoy the support of countless members of the population. Their principles are comparable to the aims of the Imam of the city of Sarh in southern Chad, who despite a thirty-year civil war in the country has worked indefatigably for reconciliation between Christians and Muslims. Despite the angry resistance of other groups he is building up informal networks of encounter and thus realizing the spiritual aims of his old mystical order of the Tijania, which according to Berndt has 'traditionally played the role of moderator and peace-keeper'.

In many places, Islam today is producing peace movements which work quietly and inconspicuously. However, they are often overshadowed by politics. The work of the Muslim Peace Fellowship, which assimilates and collects Islamic experiences of peace and non-violence, is very important. It has also been able to support the efforts of present-day Arab communities in Israel which are concerned for balance and reconciliation. Though Sheikh Nimr Darvish, leader of the 'Islamic Movement' in Palestine, rejects the terrorism of the Hamas movement, he has not yet subscribed to the principle of unconditional non-violence. But in the name of his faith – on the basis of an agreement over justice – he is pursuing a strategy of de-escalating and limiting violence. That is the minimum which can be achieved at present, and even it can only be achieved if religious motivations are mobilized. The list of Islamic leaders could be continued. I need mention only Smail Balic, the famous spokesman of Bosnian Islam, who is married to a Protestant wife and is now working for reconciliation and tolerance from Vienna.

I might mention two other writers. The first, the Sudanese author Khalid Kishtainy, is interesting because he is explicitly concerned with the Islamic heritage of non-violence. In accordance with Muslim tradition he wants to avoid the impression of a passive pacifism, remote from the world. At the same time he wants to show that the Muslim *jihad* (wrongly translated 'holy war') is quite compatible with the renunciation of violence. So he extends the traditional distinction between the '*jihad* of the heart' (confession and self-discipline) and the '*jihad* of the hand' (defence and fighting) by adding the *jihad madani*, the 'civil *jihad*'. In his view, this accurately denotes non-violent action against the present regime of his country, which scorns human rights.

The second author, the Egyptian Nasr Hamed Abu Zaid, is interesting because the Western world has only recently become aware of his fate. As the victim of the fundamentalist tendencies in his country, he fulfils all the conditions of a dissident. His marriage was forcibly broken up because his wife was not allowed to live with an 'unbelieving' heretic. For Abu Zaid, 'God is greater than all enmities'.[12] Beyond question his work, too, is rooted in his Muslim faith. He believes that the fact that all human beings are created by the one God has consequences. In his social criticism he calls for the overcoming of the gulf between poverty and riches; in his criticism of culture for equal rights for men and women; and in his criticism of religion for equal rights also for Jews and Christians and in accordance with the tradition of Sufism for respect for other religions, which are to be understood as different ways to the one God. In accordance with the Qur'an he calls for a culture of friendship between the three Abrahamic religions, and also for deep respect for Buddhism, the Hindus and the 'nature religions'. He also has a further characteristic which is indispensable for rational discussion between the religions. Patiently, in great detail and with clear arguments, he approaches the Qur'an by means of historical criticism and a careful hermeneutic. This makes it possible for him to take Allah's word seriously in a new way, by at the same time paying attention to the present situation.

4. Biblical tradition

It would take us too far here to give even a short survey of Jewish and Christian individuals and movements which have subscribed to the principles of overcoming violence and non-violence. It is sufficiently well known how intensively Jewish groups have become engaged in the project of reconciliation in present-day Israel. As a rule we know Christian groups better than dissidents from other religions. We find them in the industrialized states and in Latin America, in the countless lands of Africa and Asia, in Ireland and in Croatia, in the slums of Sao Paulo, and in the numerous initiatives for children or women, for AIDS sufferers or those who have been driven openly or in other ways from their native lands. There are indigenous individuals and movements, and often priests, members of orders or helpers from other continents. This issue of *Concilium* has already reported on the indispensable world-wide contribution of women. A whole gallery of successful or exemplary cases of non-violence has now been produced. To adopt the terminology of Christian churches, there are 'saints' whose social and political significance has been rediscovered, like Francis of Assisi and Bartolomé de Las Casas, to whom attention has been drawn by Gustavo Gutierrez; and there are Mother Teresa of Calcutta or Oscar Romero, who was shot at the altar on 24 March 1980 because of his message of non-violent criticism. He preferred to be shot rather than to fire a shot himself. Despite murder threats, two days previously he had accused the military regime of murder and acts of violence during previous weeks.

Romero referred to God's command 'You shall not kill' and continued: 'No soldier is obliged to obey an order contrary to God's command . . . No one need observe an immoral law. Now it is time to discover one's own conscience and follow it instead of the order of sin . . . An end to repression!'[13] Such words were evidently felt by the representatives of violence to be subversive. Romero was silenced. Did he achieve anything? Can violence not only be criticized but also overcome, and if so, how?

III. From criticism to the overcoming of violence

1. Concrete criticism of violence

There are many ways of criticizing violence, and many ways of overcoming violence, some obvious and some more devious. I have pointed out that the *ahimsa* of the Indian traditions has a very broad and almost natural meaning, whereas the non-violence of the prophetic religions is always confronted with the problem of shaping the world. Now our possibilities of shaping the world – improving it and manipulating it – have increased enormously. Our political and financial potential, our potential in communication, medicine, technology and weapons, is almost unlimited. Our highly sophisticated modern societies have necessitated the drawing of distinctions within the problem of violence of which the old and venerable sources of our religion had no inkling. Moreover it is becoming increasingly clear that non-violence must not be confused with passivity. Should the Jews not have resisted being sent to concentration camps the moment that the Germans imposed this fate on them? That would be an absurd notion. The overcoming of violence presupposes an active formation of consciousness, active action, and sometimes active resistance.

So theologians are often engaged in the wrong kind of discussion when they restrict themselves in a one-sided way to the exegesis of their canonical documents. Of course believers (i.e. the members of the various religions) should honour their different ideals of the criticism and overcoming of violence. Without the sources of such motivation the face of the earth will not be changed. But how can we also make the criticism of violence politically fruitful today, and thus really overcome violence? In all the religions there is a tendency to celebrate the ideal of non-violence as a great achievement, but this proves escapist when non-violence is regarded as just an ideal. Thus in Yugoslavia, neither Muslim nor Orthodox nor Catholic religious leaders had the courage to dispense with violence as a means of politics. To be enthusiastic in a general way about non-violence is therefore dangerous; since non-violence cannot be proved in an area which is free of violence, the proving must take place in a confrontation with violence which really exists and will involve sacrifice. Non-violence finds itself in crisis where the call for help and despair at the existing misery seem to go unanswered. The criticism of violence makes sense only if it begins in such situations, perhaps contrary to anything that has gone before. Indeed, the ideal of a non-violent world takes on a religious urgency only because it borders on the utopian and thus seem to have no place in the world. But does it nevertheless have a place, and if so why?

An amazing fact needs to be reported at this point: many religious and non-religious people have discovered the aim of a consistent overcoming of violence not in a preoccupation with religious writing, but in dealing with violence itself. I believe that such a development can be discovered for example in Nelson Mandela, who at the beginning of his political career still allowed sabotage as a principle of political action (but ruled out terrorism, revolt and revolution). Examples from the Christian sphere are Oscar Romero and Samuel Ruiz, the bishop of Chiapas in southern Mexico, who works on behalf of the Indios. By their own confession, both only learnt gradually, and in dealing with the oppressed themselves, for whom and how they had to act as bishops. They received small thanks from the official side. Thus those who have learned non-violence are often reluctant dissidents.

If we are to believe the testimony of such people, non-violent treatment of others has its own compelling rationality, particularly in situations of violence. The situation of suffering creates its own spiritual sources. Gustavo Gutierrez has described much of this rationality.[14] Many years previously the German theologian Dorothee Sölle said a great deal about it, recalling the mystic Meister Eckart, when she was writing about the blind young Frenchman Jacques Lusseyran, who became the focus of truth for many of those in Auschwitz. There is an acceptance, an adoption of suffering, which has nothing to do with masochism but makes it possible to overcome suffering.[15] So the important thing is not that there is a biblical, an Indian or any other canonical text which teaches power in suffering, but that such texts open our eyes to this experience. In this experience there is a worldwide ecumene of dissidents. And the dissidents of all the religions of the world to whom such experience is given have a common function. They present the spirituality of non-violence as an attitude which has the utmost social and political significance. Through them this common heritage of the religions becomes evident as a shared obligation.

2. Experience and analysis

However, there is still much work to be done to achieve understanding and enlightenment. 'Non-violence' understood as a way and a goal needs not only spiritual experience but also rational, analytical investigation. Here at least three aspects need to be noted.

The first has already been mentioned. It relates to the various frameworks of reference within which the religions speak of violence and non-violence. Indian *ahimsa* is based on the order of human beings in the world and nature; it tends towards remoteness from the world, a passive farewell to the world and reality. Gandhi opposed this tendency and was therefore criticized by Hindus. In certain circumstances he even allowed the killing of a calf, and in an emergency allowed violence against other human beings.[16] Here Gandhi reinforced a very dynamic and often forgotten basic feature of Hindu religions, the sense of the drama of good and evil which is embodied in good and demonic gods. This runs contrary to an all-too-passive and fatalistic understanding of *karma*. The same goes for Buddhism. Impulses within Buddhism which are opposed to violence can easily come close to denying suffering and to an asceticism which turns away from the world. Therefore Maha Ghosananda and Omalpe Sobhita Thero, also to the disapproval of many of their collegaues, spoke of the temples of human experience. The introduction of the civil *jihad*, which adds a much more positive and certainly unusual emphasis to the aspect of defence and perfecting the self, is also a subject for serious discussion.[17]

The second aspect follows from what has already been said. It is the global and globalized framework of our common present. The dimensions of violence have increased all over the world and rest on a disturbing and complex network of material, cultural and social factors. Cause and effect often cannot be identified. In certain situations the reduction of violence can provoke explosions of violence; in other situations the recollection of violence prevents the construction of a non-violent future. The renunciation of violence perhaps appears only in the gradual demolition of violence; perhaps true non-violence can only achieve a clear asymmetry of violence and counter-violence. Even Jesus drove the merchants out of the temple court, and said that he was bringing the sword. This new and tremendously complex situation[18] calls for new efforts of translation almost every day. Thus for example in the German Pax Christi movement there is once again a discussion of the question whether, given a new world situation, non-violence is to be understood afresh as a prime and absolute option. This problem can hardly be resolved theoretically. Real non-violence presupposes not only political and social experience but also a concrete competence in conflict and peace – which is constantly threatened and has constantly to be attained afresh. All this rests on religious roots and must therefore be worked out afresh in the religions.

There is also a need for a debate on the question how we can assimilate and overcome not only the present situations of violence but also the apocalyptic histories of violence in the twentieth century generally. How difficult that is can be seen from the damage done by German Fascism, which still has not been healed. So the written documentation and assimilation of crimes in Brazil which Cardinal Arns initiated in 1979 is of prime importance.[19] Here I also have in mind the Truth and Reconciliation Commission under the chairmanship of Bishop Desmond Tutu, which was set up by the Republic of South Africa in July 1995 to address the crimes committed under the apartheid regime. Here the intention is not to humiliate the perpetrators but to reinstate the victims, leading to acknowledgement, confession and reconciliation. Such necessary processes, too, can hardly succeed without a religious competence in confronting terror and without the primal religious competence of forgiveness.

Conclusion: No to violence

This article has produced several important results which I shall sum up in five ponts.
1. All religions are critical of violence, though the frameworks of this criticism differ widely. At the same time, all religions know tendencies in which the practice of violence is unconditionally rejected.
2. In all religions there are individuals or groups today which are working in the name of their religion and in concrete situations for reconciliation, for overcoming or abolishing violence. These individuals and groups often work with non-religious, e.g. with politically or socially orientated, groups.
3. Such movements regularly prompt debates within their own tradition because they criticize and extend their own traditions with a view to the present. They undeniably raise the question of the spirit and topicality of canonical texts over and above a literal exegesis.
4. The way from mental repudiation of violence to real overcoming of it cannot be decreed theoretically, but must be attempted practically. Here rational analysis of social conditions in addition to concrete commitment is indispensable.
5. There is a religious competence for non-violence and overcoming violence which derives directly from solidarity with the victims of violence. This concept can be extremely significant for social policy in settling conflicts, confronting injustice, forgiveness and the advancement of trust.

Finally, to return to a basic question: the theoretical alternative 'non-violence or not' does not go far enough, as we have already seen. Nevertheless the situation in the world compels us to draw new boundaries. Because of our technological potential and the interconnection of the whole world, the question of violence within and betwen states has taken on new urgency. The question is a very simple one: given the present possibilities, is the use of violence still acceptable at all as a way of settling conflicts within and between states? The answer must be that resolving conflict generally by violence is no longer acceptable today, since the extent and intensity of the violence can no longer be calculated and it may result in the destruction of whole spheres of life. As Gandhi said in the 1920s and the Declaration of the Parliament of the World's Religions said in 1993, the world is in agony. The universal commandment of the religions, 'You shall not kill', is therefore of absolute and world-wide urgency. In principle all the great religions have understood this.[20] But they have understood it only in principle and their mutual readiness for reconciliation has not been able to produce global peace. So it is important finally to elevate the general obligation to world peace to a religious and political awareness that is politically effective.

Translated by John Bowden.

Notes

1. H. Küng and J. Ching, *Christianity and Chinese Religions*, New York and London 1989; H. Maspero, *Taoism and Chinese Religion*, Amherst 1981.

2. J. Kuttianical, 'Non-violence the Core of Religious Experience in Gandhi', *Journal of Dharma* 14, 1989, 227–45. The author makes generalized references to Jainism and Buddhism, especially to the Upanishads and the Bhagavadgita. In addition, in Gandhi's own words there is a discussion of 1. the American H. D. Thoreau and his essay 'Resistance to Civil Government' (1849), later 'On the Duty of Civil Disobedience' (1849); 2. the Englishman John Ruskin and his book *Onto This Last. Four Essays on the First Principles of Political Economy* (1862); 3. the work of Leo Tolstoy and 4. The Sermon on the Mount.

3. H. Bechert, 'Buddhist Perspectives', in H. Küng et al., *Christianity and the World Religions. Paths of Dialogue with Islam, Hinduism and Buddhism*, New York and London 1986, 291–305: 229; D. L. and J. T. Carmody, *Serene Compassion: A Christian Appreciation of Buddhist Holiness*, New York 1996; E. Frauwallner, *Die Philosophie des Buddhismus*, Berlin [4]1994; P. Harvey, *An Introduction to Buddhism: Teachings, History and Practices*, Cambridge 1990.

4. J. van Ess, 'Islamic Perspectives', in Kung et al., *Christianity and the World Religions* (n. 4), 70–82: 72; A. Rippin, *Muslims. Their Religious Beliefs and Practices, I: The Formative Period*, London 1990.

5. R. Gramlich, *Alte Vorbilder des Sufitums* (2 vols.), Wiesbaden 1995/96; V. J. Hoffman, *Sufism, Mystics, and Saints in Modern Egypt*, Columbia 1995; Rippin, *Muslims* (n. 5), 117–28: A. Schimmel, *Mystical Dimensions of Islam*, Chapel Hill 1975; R. C. Zaehner, *Hindu and Muslim Mysticism*, New York 1960.

6. These distinctions play a major role for Gandhi, who is central to the modern discussion of non-violence (Kuttianical, 'Non-violence the Core of Religious Experience' [n. 2], 234–7).

7. H. Küng has worked this out and summarized it in classical fashion in *Credo, The Apostles' Creed Explained for Today*, London and New York 1993, 51–6 ('What Jesus and Gautama have in common', 'Where Jesus and Gautama differ', 'The Illuminated and the Crucified').

8. G. Lohfink, *Jesus and the Community. The Social Dimension of Christian Faith*, Philadelphia and London 1982, 181–203; quotation from the letter to Diognetus.

9. Those Protestants were originally called 'dissidents' who from 1573 on were tolerated in the then Catholic state. The 'Dissenters' or 'Nonconformists' were originally those religious groups which did not join the Church of England in 1660.

10. One of the great dissidents of that time, who despite his good relations with religious groups uses purely secular arguments, is Nelson Mandela, now President of the Republic of South Africa (N. Mandela, *The Struggle is my Life: His Speeches and Writings brought together with Historical Documents and Accounts of Mandela in Prison by Fellow-Prisoners*, London 1990; id., *Nelson Mandela Speaks: Speeches, Statements and Articles*, London 1991; id., *I am Prepared to Die*, London 1964). The power of religious motivation can be recognized in theologians like A. Boesak ('The Relationship between Text and Situation, Reconciliation and Liberation in Black Theology', in *Voices of the Third World* 2, 1979, no. 1, 34–40); M. Buthelezi ('Violence and the Cross in South Africa', in *Journal of Theology for Southern Africa* 29, December 1979, 51–5; Bishop D. Tutu (*The Voice of One Crying in the Wilderness: A Collection of Recent Statements in the Struggle for Justice in Africa*, London 1982), or the Catholic priest and respected ANC politician and Vice President of the Parliament of the Republic of South Africa, Smangaliso Mkhatswha, who was imprisoned for a long time and tortured because of his non-violent resistance (Interview 'Wie der Frieden über die Gewalt siegt', *Publik-Forum* 24, 1995, no. 6, 10–11).

11. Here I am using throughout the report by H. Berndt, 'Für das Gute um die Wette streiten', *Publik-Forum* 25, 1996, No. 9, 29–30.

12. 'Gott ist grösser als alle Feindschaften', interview with T. Seiterich-Kreuzkamp, *Publik-Forum* 25, 1996, No. 1, 12 January 1996, 3–34.

13. A. O. Romero, '*!Cese la represión!*', Madrid 1980, 205; id., 'The Church and Popular Political Organizations. From the Third Pastoral Letter of Archbishop Romero', *Voices from the Third World* 14, 1991, 108–35.

14. G. Gutiérrez, *We Drink from Our Own Wells. The Spiritual Journey of a People*, Maryknoll and London 1984; id., *On Job. God-Talk and the Suffering of the Innocent*, Maryknoll 1987; J. Van Nieuwenhove, *Bronnen van bevrijding. Varianten in de theologie van Gustavo Gutiérrez*, Kampen 1991.

15. J. Lusseyran, *Das wiedergefundene Licht*, Hamburg 1971; D. Sölle, *Suffering*, London 1973, 112–18. This is also reported by Nelson Mandela, who in the worst periods of his imprisonment still succeeded in discovering a glimmer of humanity in his guards. That was enough to help him go on living.

16. M. K. Gandhi, *Non-Violence in Peace and War*, Ahmedabad, reprint 1962; id., *My Non-Violence*. Ahmedabad 1960; T. Merton (ed.), *Gandhi on Non-Violence. A Selection from the Writings of Mahatma Gandhi*, Toronto 1965; H. Bürkle, 'Ein indisches Ideal im modernen Kontext: *ahimsa*', in U. Bianchi (ed.), *The Notion of 'Religion' in Comparative Research. Selected Proceedings of the XVI JAHR Congress*, Rome 1993, 787–95; V. P. Gaur, *Mahatma Gandhi. A Study of his Message of Non-Violence*, New Delhi 1977; Kuttianical, 'Non-violence the Core of Religious Experience' (n. 2); U. Tahtinen, *Ahimsa. Non-Violence in Indian Tradition*, London 1976.

17. Abdullahi Ahmed An-Na'im, 'Qur'an, Shari'a and Human Rights: Foundations, Deficiencies and Prospects', *Concilium* 1990/2, 61–9. One major problem of understanding between Christianity and Islam seems to be that Islam derives its legitimation for fighting from a situation of inferiority and the pressure to self-preservation. Like Muhammad, Islam will not give up without a fight. Of course the death of Jesus presents another paradigm. However, the position in Islam does not prevent criticism of violence any more than the death of Jesus in Christianity prevents metaphors related to fighting: Eph. 6.13; Phil. 1.30; Col. 2.1; I Tim. 1.18; 6.12; II Tim. 4.7.

18. G. Gutiérrez, 'The Violence of a System', *Concilium* 140, 1980, 93–100; E. Lascaris, 'De medemens als model en obstakel. De hypothese van René Girard en haar betekenis voor de theologie', *Tijdschrift voor Theologie* 24, 1984, 115–37; C. J.

Pinto de Oliveira, 'Het gebruik van geweld in de strijd tegen onrechtvaardige structuren', in: *Concilium* 14, 1978, no. 10, 89–103 (not in English).

19. The proceedings have grown to twelve volumes amounting to almost 7,000 pages. An abbreviated edition has appeared under the title *Brasil nunca mais: un relato para a historia*, Petropolis 1985.

20. H. W. Gensichen, *Weltreligionen und Weltfriede*, Göttingen 1985; C. H. Ratschow (ed.), *Ethik der Religionen. Ein Handbuch*, Stuttgart 1980.

Violence as an Anthropological Constant? Towards a New Evaluation

Jean Pierre Wils

It may hardly seem surprising today, at the end of a century steeped in blood, that violence is a genuine phenomenon of human history and cannot merely be dismissed as an occasional deviation. What is more surprising is the delay in stating this sober diagnosis. Given the pedagogical optimism about the possibility of educating the human race at the time of the Enlightenment, as represented by Lessing, the statement reflects some disappointment. It indicates the global disillusionment after the catastrophes which have befallen humankind this century: for the moment, the great projects of humanity have been suspended. But even the more modest variant of that optimism, namely the possibility of changing the individual 'for the better', is coming up against considerable credibility problems. The debate over whether therapy works with sexual offenders, which has become so vigorous as a result of the brutal murder of children, makes it clear that there is a kind of biological or genetic resistance to the pedagogical-therapeutic reshaping of behaviour patterns. Here too the optimists about education are almost sneaking off the field.

What was attributed thirty years ago to the influence of the environment is now increasingly being attributed to genetic characteristics. Even if we are not to commit the opposite mistake, that of attributing everything to a natural genetic determinism,[1] we cannot avoid accepting changes in the balance of power between 'nature' and 'culture'. At any rate the reservoir of natural conditioning, which to a large degree is determined, may be taken to have increased in content and depth, whereas the power of factors leading towards civilization and culture needs to be assessed more realistically or more modestly. The needle of freedom goes on stitching its artistic pattern, but the material on which it stitches has become coarser and more resistant, and is reluctant to yield to good and beautiful intentions. The figure which is produced proves to be a fluke, and the distorted results a sorry norm.

This analysis becomes particularly oppressive when it proves that 'aggressiveness' as a potential biological drive is in turn a dominant cultural factor. Whereas Freud could still refer to the 'potential for sublimation' as a force which creates culture, today attention must be drawn once again to the suppressed premises, to the refractory present of what is sublimated, namely to aggression itself.

Here it must be said that in an anthropological approach the legal and political concept of violence ('the state's monopoly of violence', 'legal violence') stands in the foreground. In such a perspective, violence always has to be associated with 'acts of violence', 'destructiveness' and 'brutality'.

In regulating themselves externally, cultures display deeply rooted 'exclusive' demarcations which can be interpreted as the expressions of directed, collective aggressiveness.[2] And even the internal potential for restraining violence has had only limited success in pacification. If we look at the geopolitical landscape of Europe, we cannot avoid diagnosing regular eruptions of semi-collective and collective violence. At present Albania shows how quickly disappointments (and manifest self-deception) can lead to completely uncontrollable escapades of violence which cannot be directed by any 'project' or ideology. The prophetic predictions of Hans Magnus Enzenberger in his 'Views of the Civil War'[3] are being fulfilled precisely; we have the maraudings of anarchical power which can even put in question the biological maxims of self-preservation.

'Aggressiveness' as the biological nucleus of violence

If we are talking here of an 'anthropological' constant, it is natural to look for indications of the human potential for violence in anthropology itself. For it cannot have escaped the interested gaze of anthropologists that their object, in which they themselves are of course included, has not only caring and peaceful tendencies but also aggressive drives. By 'anthropology' here I mean that theoretical attitude which makes an empirical and speculative examination of human beings – empirical in the sense of an orientation by real experiences, and speculative in the sense of a synthesis of these experiences in a (provisional) picture. So here we are not concerned with the late philosophical discipline or early ethnology.

The misanthropy expressed in Joseph de Maistre's view that human beings are nothing but a disease[4] is a corrective to what is suppressed in all smooth and optimistic approaches – precisely because of all its hyperbole. The anthropofugal traditions which run from Blaise Pascal to Eduard von Hartmann, Arthur Koestler, Günther Anders and Cioran always kept alive the recollection that under the veneer of civilization a gaping abyss of bestiality and violence opens up. Perhaps the most fundamental and most important correction of this omnipresence of violence begins where the knowledge of the violent nature of human beings is not sacrificed to an abstract philosophy.

However, no comfort can be found in the animal world either: in many places the view prevails that animals in particular do not kill out of cruelty or sheer aggression, but only because they are hungry. The way in which animals limit violence to a degree necessary for survival and the derivation of violence from the 'functional mass' of aggressiveness raise hopes that in a kind of evolutionary recollection of their buried animality, human beings might conceivably limit their violence. However, this too has proved to be an illusion. The Dutch ethologist Frans de Waal, famous throughout the world for his research into primates, had to point out in a book entitled *Good Natured*, that animals quite often kill for sheer aggression which has no function and for delight in the suffering of others. And if we are right in attributing a kind of proto-morality to chimpanzees, this should not lead us to forget that it is precisely the capacity for this morality which at the same time makes possible the deep amorality of killing for killing's sake. The subtitle of de Waal's book is, 'On the origins of good and evil in human beings and other animals'.[5] Those beginnings of awareness, which are necessary for proto-moral behaviour, at the same time unleash energies for amoral behaviour.

At all events, the thesis still put forward by B. Hassenstein, that all aggressiveness in animals has a well-defined biological function,[6] seems increasingly to be on the wane. Biologically dysfunctional aggressive behaviour is undeniable not only among human beings but also among animals.

Now we can attempt to define violence as biologically and culturally dysfunctional aggressiveness. Where all mechanisms and forms of self-preservation and the preservation of others have no biological or cultural function, in that aggressiveness does not serve either the needs of hunger or the needs of defence, either procreation or the establishment of a hierarchy, either the legitimate defence of the next generation or the diversion of drives into play, we can talk of violence.

But the very concept of dysfunction is already an indication of how to deal with violence. Paul Watzlawick has formulated a principle related to human forms of communication which allows the identification of 'pathogenic' forms:

> Pathological systems do not have sufficient metarules, i.e. rules for changing their rules. It should immediately be clear that such a system

cannot cope with a system for which its rules (its repertoire of behaviour) are inadequate, nor can it produce new rules or alter existing rules to cope with the particular situation. Rather, such a system is caught in a vicious circle which we call a game without end.[7]

This descriptive and systematic description has the advantage of offering both biological and determined factors for aggression and cultural mechanisms for directing it. Moreover it avoids over-hasty assessments and thus corrects the one-sidedly negative semantics.

Accordingly, 'aggressiveness' can be interpreted as behaviour which follows the rules, to the degree that the functions mentioned above are purposively fulfilled. By contrast 'violence' could be described as a deregulated form of behaviour. If we look at the relation between the sexes, its aggressive basic structure cannot be denied. Sexuality as a brute fact, and also its erotic transformations, cannot be imagined without a foundation of desire and aggression. However, this foundation is subject to ongoing and far-reaching cultural changes. And as soon as a particular form of the relationship between the sexes avoids new and serious challenges by refusing to reconsider the validity of the old rules, the regulated aggressiveness is deregulated. Aggressiveness which is not directed by culture turns into violence. Accordingly both biological and cultural components are bound up with this concept.

The by no mean random suspending of particular rules, which in principle is always possible, must therefore be understood as an important presupposition for a culture which, if it is not without aggression, is certainly non-violent. The discovery of new rules will presumably have to follow what Watzlawick calls 'metarules', which make it possible to find cognitive strategies for the resolution of moral conflicts. If for example the traditional rules governing the relations between the sexes require substantial expansion or call for new forms of life, then in my view principles of justice should come in as 'metarules'. In this way 'alternative biologisms' can be avoided as new 'natural' foundations for those relationships.

Ambiguities in the phenomenon and uncertainties in ethical judgment

Violence is defined as dysfunctional aggressive behaviour. Now not only in our own culture but also in other cultures we encounter institutions and practices which cannot clearly be called aggression or violence. For example, sado-masochism represents a mixed form: it increases the latently aggressive behaviour which is contained in any sexual practice as part of a complex event. Aggression becomes obvious. Sado-masochistic practices transcend all *prima facie* functions of sexuality. But they demonstrate – albeit in an extreme form – that human sexuality (and not only that) always has dysfunctional features. So sexuality cannot in any way be reduced to a strategy of the self-preservation of the species. And since eroticism quite often has self-destructive features, we have to concede that the game of destruction and cruelty which is set up does not represent violence in the real sense. This only superficially paradoxical mixture of enjoyment and pain, of desire and suffering, produces an intermediate world in which the fantasy of cruelty and the desire for pain cannot be described adequately either as functional aggressiveness or as an expression of unfettered violence. Rather, we have the taming of violence by means of the staging of violence.

Of course here we are entering a borderline area which is not without risk and danger. But within the framework of a realistic anthropology we cannot evade such a phenomenon. Here it must be noted that it is precisely the ethical evaluation of such phenomena, difficult though it is to carry out with certainty, which causes them to divert into the sphere of art and ethics. Here the ethical verdict may be taken to be suspended. But how can we at least hint at a basis for this judgment?

I think that Georges Bataille developed a usable model in his famous article on 'Sovereignty'. Bataille answered the question how the 'animal' violence in human beings which manifests itself in sexuality and in the experience of dying and death can be combined with the capacity for reflection, for distancing, with the complementary terms 'prohibition' and 'transgression'. Here 'prohibition' stands for the taming power of reflection which results in distancing, while 'transgression' stands for the transcendent power of the animal.

> What confuses us most is that at the level of the prohibition human dignity rises above the animal, but at the level of transgression, which is the nature of the sacral, the animal appears holier than the human being (animals are often fused with gods): the transgression is essentially a return, albeit regulated and subject to limits, to the animal drive which has become divine.[8]

In the history of religion it is certain that sexuality and death are two anthropological constants the regulation of which is ambivalent. The numerous prescriptions and tabu rules bear eloquent testimony to the degree to which these two latently unregulated phenomena, which indeed transcend rules, must be tamed through prohibition, reflection and moral interiorization. A community which finds no rules for sexuality and death will fall apart. It is not a community. It becomes the victim of sheer violence. Nevertheless, by way of compensation, room is made for a transgression of the prohibition in particular places and at ritually defined times. Whereas, for example, in every religion death is surrounded by prohibitions, tabus over contact and distancing techniques, it is constantly brought back in the context of well-defined scenes. In particular the Catholic variant of the eucharist is a way of dealing with the 'blood' and 'body' of death, which for the recipient results in an identification that shows features of self-dissolution: it is the old self which in the eucharist makes room for the self of another who has already gone beyond life and vicariously overcome death. Far be it for me to reduce the eucharist to this structure, but no interpretation, however sublime and theologically sensitive, can avoid an anthropological sub-structure. It is not completely wrong to discover surviving elements of cruelty and death in the eucharist. This is a ritual feeding on the bringer of salvation. But just as it would be wrong to reduce the eucharist to a reprehensible manifestation of violence – e.g. as secret cannibalism – so it would be wrong not to want to see any signs of violence in it. However, this violence is now overcome symbolically, transformed into an aggressiveness which is tolerable. Certain religious rites can be understood as functional stagings of aggressiveness.

> There is in us a sovereign, overwhelming illumination which we generally regard as being most desirable and which evades the clear awareness in which anything has its place for us: so much so that human life consists of two heterogeneous parts which never unite. One is meaningful, and its meaning lies in useful goals which are systematically subordinated: this part we are conscious of. The other is sovereign: it is occasionally formed by an unruliness of the first; it is dark, or rather bright, but it blinds, and thus at all events evades the consciousness. So the problem is twofold. The consciousness wants to extend its rule to violence. On the other hand the violence seeks beyond itself for consciousness.[9]

Against the background of this anthropology, numerous phenomena which display aggressive and/or violent features can be subjected to a more cautious assessment than is often the case in direct examinations with a moral loading. Here I shall begin from the necessity of anthropological reflections for ethics: without a sufficiently complex anthropology, ethical statements are literally left hanging. Even if one does not doubt the validity of the naturalistic fallacy for explanatory models in principle, one has to combine the chances of a realistic ethic with the context-function of anthropology. In particular the aggressive elements attached to the topics of sexuality and death will then have to be seen in a more subtle way, so that the ethical judgment can also be refined. It will be possible to gain a more adequate picture for the phenomenology of religion, over and above its aggressive and violent aspects. Where there are no techniques for transformation and no rules for systems to represent the aggressive elements of sexuality and death, this potential goes astray and is uncontrolled. Where the covetous aggressive elements in religions are not recognized or denied, the same thing happens.

In Jean Baudrillard's reflections on the philosophy of culture, the greatest importance is attached to the need to give sufficient space to the equivalence of Eros and Thanatos (to use Freud's terms). For Baudrillard, the 'symbolic exchange', in the sense of a reference to these through the senses and ritual, is a way of depicting the dialectical interweaving of consciousness and violence, reflection and aggressiveness, prohibition and transgression. The diagnosis is that a culture of simulation which has banished all remaining sensual references to reality from its sign-system in the long run risks falling victim to the manifestations of aggression which have become uncontrollable and therefore violent.[10]

But how is it possible to ensure that a culture which gives a symbolic space to aggressiveness can effectively and permanently safeguard itself from violence? How can we guarantee that the symbol systems are not so vulnerable and delicate that they collapse with only a little cultural shaking? Has not the emergence of civil wars even in Central Europe shown sufficiently how fragile worlds of symbols are? To take up Walter Benjamin's question, 'Is it at all possible for conflicts to be settled non-violently?'

At this point there is no avoiding recourse to the legal concept of violence. On the contrary, just as Bataille couples the sphere of the 'prohibition' dialectically with aggression by means of the concept of 'transgression', so one could regard the legal and political concept of violence – the core of any theory of democracy – as a normative manifestation of functional aggressiveness because it is regulated. It can be designated 'aggressiveness for the purpose of establishing legitimate order'. Precisely because democratic forms of the state accord this 'ordered aggression' a place with norms and functions in 'finding consensus by means of dissent', in that it is tolerated as a means of forming opinion and making decisions, unlike dictatorships they are in a position to build up structure of peaces both inwardly and outwardly. By contrast, the violent repression of any functional 'ordered violence' as a systematic means of policy is a characteristic of the violence in dictatorships: terrorizing opinions and dispositions as a means of total 'pacification inwards' on the one hand, and transforming opponents into enemies and deliberately liquidating them on the other, form the violent face of this prevention of 'ordered aggression'.

Nevertheless we have to go one stage further. Any manifestation of aggression, however violent, has a prior basis, namely a particular view of the world. Benjamin replies to the question of the possibility of the non-violent resolution of conflicts as follows:

> Certainly. Relations between private individuals are full of examples of this. Non-violent agreement can be found wherever the culture of the heart has given people pure means of agreement. Non-violent means are pure means to set over against any kind of means, whether in accordance with the law or contrary to the law, which are utterly violent. Courtesy, affection, friendship, trust and other things are their subjective presupposition. But their objective manifestation is governed by the law that pure means are never direct solutions but are always indirect solutions. So they never relate directly to the resolution of interpersonal conflicts, but only do so through the issues.[11]

Precisely because this form of arbitration avoids that detour which is necessary in the sphere of law, it develops a network of direct communication through the senses. So it can be claimed 'that there is a human agreement in the sphere of non-violence that is completely inaccessible to violence: the real sphere of "agreement", namely language'.

Although language represents a world of symbols in which words can kill, it is impossible to go behind it, as one can with other symbolic worlds, or to destroy it, as long as cultures exist at all. If talking is 'fighting' and manifests combative elements, as Lyotard remarks,[12] language is a semantic locus of aggressive human self-communication. The rhetorical use, but far more the demagogic misuse, of language knows this function very well. For the same reason, however, it is an agreement which is unavoidable for a symbolic world: the issue is disputed vicariously because it is disputed symbolically. Therefore language is always an agreement about aggressions, even where these are not directly the topic. In the language of morality, but *a fortiori* in the morality of language itself, we find those elements which can fix the boundary between aggressiveness and violence.

Notes

1. Cf. S. J. Gould, *Der falsch vermessene Mensch*, Frankfurt 1988, 359ff.
2. Cf. S. P. Huntington, *The Clash of Civilisations*, New York 1996.
3. Hans Magnus Enzensberger, *Aussichten auf den Bürgerkrieg*, Frankfurt 1993.
4. Josèphe de Maistre, *L'homme entier n'est qu'une maladie*, Paris 1960 edition, 56.
5. I have used the Dutch edition, *Van nature goed. Over de oorsprong van goed en kwaad in mensen en andere dieren*, Amsterdam and Antwerp 1996, esp. 101ff.

6. 'Das spezifisch Menschliche nach den Resultaten der Verhaltensforschung', in *Neue Anthropologie*, ed. H. Gadamer and P. Vogler, Vol. 2, *Biologische Anthropologie. Zweiter Teil*, Stutgart 1972, 60–97.

7. P. Watzlawick, 'Wesen und Formen menschlicher Beziehungen', in *Neue Anthropologie* (n. 6), Vol. 7, *Philosophische Anthropologie, Zweiter Teil*, Stuttgart 1975, 103–131: 122.

8. *Die psychologische Struktur des Faschismus. Die Souveranitat*, ed. E. Lenk, Munich 1978, 52.

9. G. Bataille, 'Sade und der normale Mensch', in: id., *Der heilige Eros*, Frankfurt, Berlin and Vienna 1979, 174–193: 190. Cf. id., 'Die Aufhebung der Ökonomie', in *Das theoretische Werk*, I, ed. G. Bergfleht, Munich 1975. There is a good account in G. Häfliger, *Autonomie oder Souveranität. Zur Gegenwartskritik von Georges Bataille*, Mittenwald 1981; also J. Habermas, 'Zwischen Erotismus und Gewalt', in *Der philosophische Diskurs der Moderne*, Frankfurt 1985, 248–79.

10. *Der symbolische Tausch und der Tod*, Munich 1982, 80ff.

11. 'Zur Kritik der Gewalt', in *Gesammelte Schriften* 11.1, ed. R. Tiedemann and H. Schweppenhauser, Frankfurt 1977, 179–203: 191.

12. *Der Widerstreit*, Munich 1989.

Religion as the Foundation of an Ethic of Overcoming Violence

Raymond Schwager

The world of the religions is very varied and associated with phenomena of violence in many ways. Therefore there can be no simple answer to the question how religion can be the basis for an ethic of overcoming violence. There is even a prior question: do the religions want to overcome violence at all? God, deities or gods often appear as annihilating powers and they quite often instigate people to kill others. Thus Yahweh commands his people whom he has led out of Egypt to exterminate the seven peoples in Palestine (Deut. 7.1–26), and in the Bhagavadgita the incarnate god (avatar) Krishna resolutely summons the commander Arjuna, who does not want to fight against his own kinsfolk, to war: 'If you are defeated, you will win heaven. But if you are victorious, you will enjoy earth. Therefore arise, O son of Kunti, resolutely for battle' (II, 37). In practice there have been other 'holy' wars in all religions, and similar notions influence the Western world even today.[1] Do the religions in which many people find supreme spiritual truths at the same time encourage violence?

1. Public order

Whether religions are thought to be a force for peace or to be aggressive largely depends on how one estimates the capacity of human beings to live together peacefully. If one believes this capacity to be great, one will spontaneously attribute the many acts of violence and wars to some dark powers by which peaceable men and women are led astray. In that case the religions belong among the powers which threaten. Such a view inspired the European Enlightenment. After the bitter experiences of the wars of religion some people thought that it was only necessary to suppress the religions from public life for a time of peace to dawn. Only different forms of nationalism took the place of the religions, and since then atrocities have been committed in the name of reason, racist nationalism or atheistic Communism which have exceeded the former misdeeds of the religions rather than fallen short of them.

Already long before the Enlightenment there were the beginnings of a public way of thinking which no longer wanted to ground public order directly in religion. Christoph Meier has investigated the origin of this thought in ancient Greece; he shows how there are insights above all in Aeschylus which corresponded very closely to political events of the time and are therefore more realistic than the political theories of Plato or Aristotle. However, in the tragedian the vengeful deities become peaceful beings only on the following condition:

> Friendship (*philia*) at home and unanimous hostility abroad. The reciprocity of friendship is to replace the reciprocity of murder. There is no longer to be enmity at home, but closed ranks against outsiders: a new division between friend and enemy is going to take place which is related to the *polis*, a shift in the friend-foe constellation. This is how the *polis* is to achieve its unity.[2]

This view does not just correspond to the old Greek experience; it will have changed little even in recent times. The order in human society was never taken for granted. States have always kept order by the monopoly of violence – through soldiers, the judicial system and police – and in critical situations they have above all made wars on enemies or conjured up enemies so as to weld together their own population better. The experience after the Enlightenment that the suppression of religion from public life did not produce greater peace is therefore not surprising. The problem lay deeper. But what role can the religions play in view of these political facts? Is their influence limited to reinforcing the motives of human action which are already there independently of the religions, in the direction of aggressiveness or efforts for peace?

2. Religious containment of violence

Against the background of the long experience that unity among human beings is achieved most easily by giving them common enemies, René Girard developed a precise theory about the connection between religion and violence. According to this view public religion and the social order belonged seamlessly together in archaic tribal societies (before the formation of states).[3] Because human beings are passionate creatures, violence cannot be limited only by reason. But usually it contains itself – and this is a decisive point for Girard. Disturbances and collective aggressions can easily turn into the action of all against one, and peace is regained at the cost of a victim (the scapegoat mechanism). This process takes place unnoticed because in the excitement of violence people completely lose themselves in confused projections and ecstasy. That is precisely the way in which sacral notions also arise. All the collective aggressions about a single victim are gathered together, and then all the projections about him are also concentrated. Therefore this victim appears to the excited mob as the incarnation of all evil, but at the same time also as a 'miraculous' bringer of salvation, since through their unanimous killing of him in a way which is 'inexplicable' to those involved, the reciprocal aggression has disappeared and the danger has been averted. The diametrically opposed experiences of the mob – ecstatic violence and sudden peace – transform the victim and make this victim seem both accursed and beneficial at the same time, i.e. sacral.

According to this view, in pre-state societies public religion serves not to overcome violence but to contain it. The sphere which is pacified comes about through the instinctive diversion of aggression outwards and thus through the division between sacred and profane. The sacral terror which feeds on the recollection of past danger is meant to preserve the inner sphere from the return of the threatening and the sacral, i.e. confused aggressiveness, by tabu regulations. In addition, in ritual sacrifices the original excitement and release is regularly re-enacted in a controlled way in order once again to share in its purifying effect.

The religious containment of violence (through the scapegoat mechanism, sacralization, tabu regulations and ritual sacrifices) was of vital importance in pre-state societies. Only in this way could communities which did not yet have any authority with a monopoly of violence be preserved from destroying themselves. But with the 'invention' of the state a decisive change took place, though mostly also step by step. Responsibility for public order now accrued to the central authority, which alone could use force in a legitimate way and had to suppress all other forms of violence. Whereas the opposition between sacral and profane violence was central in the pre-state community, for the state it was the ethical and political distinction between legitimate and illegitimate force that became most significant. The religions were in this way freed from direct concern for public order and therefore – thanks to new experiences of the numinous – could begin to develop independently. At the same time they largely served to preserve public order by lending a sacral aura to the authority of the state, supporting the distinction between legitimate and illegitimate violence and therefore often calling for acts of legitimate violence.

Despite Krishna's summons to battle, the Bhagavadgita does not delight in war. Rather, the problem which has just been described finds classic expression in it. It seeks to lead people to ultimate unity with the divine and to true peace. But it regards war as inevitable for the sake of public order and to punish evildoers, and therefore expects the commander (and the soldiers) to make an extremely inward distinction. They are to go boldly into battle to perform their social task, but at the same time to rid themselves of all passions. They are to overcome any desire for victory and any feeling of hatred and enmity towards opponents in their hearts. This subtle distinction between the social and the spiritual task makes a high, indeed superhuman, demand, but in one way or another it can be found in all the more universal religions. Thus for example Israel is often admonished by prophets to expect its salvation not from military strength but only from unconditional faith in Yahweh, and nevertheless to go boldly into battle. However, the distinction between social and spiritual task could easily go wrong and lead to many errors. Instead of overcoming hatred and enmity, in such cases religious inspiration tended to stir up these feelings even more. Therefore any religion must constantly ask itself how it can defend itself against such aberrations and to what behaviour it wants to inspire its adherents in critical and difficult situations.

3. The giving of love and the overcoming of violence

Do religions serve only to stem the dangerous epidemic of violence as far as possible through sacral mechanisms and through ethical and political distinctions, or is there also in them a force which really helps to overcome destructive power? As aggressions have a very deep effect on human emotions and there spontaneously combine with religious feelings and sexual strivings, the question of the overcoming of violence goes to the centre of any religion. So the following reflections must leave a general history of religions perspective and go over to a specifically Christian view.

Jesus was active within the Jewish tradition, for which it was decisive for all powers hostile to God to be overcome. Faith in Yahweh knew two ways of achieving this: the destruction of enemies and/or their conversion (cf. Zeph. 3.9f. Mal. 1.11; Isa. 60.1–5). The deepest insight into the way of conversion is offered by the Servant songs, which through a variety of dramatic roles depict how God inspires all Israel or a prophet to new conduct in the face of danger which threatens and thus sets off a process which involves others. In the first song God himself speaks and proclaims that he is putting his spirit on the Servant, so that he works indefatigably for what is right, does not cry out, does not break the bruised reed and does not quench the dimly burning wick (Isa. 42.1–4). Then the Servant himself speaks and confesses that God wakens and opens his ear anew every day so that he is capable of not defending himself and turning his back on the enemy (Isa. 50.4–6). Finally people speak who observe the fate of the Servant and experience change. First of all they think that God himself has smitten the despised Servant (Isa. 53.4). But then they note the surprising behaviour of the Servant, who is led mute as a lamb to the slaughter, and through conversion they gain a completely new perspective. Now they discover that the violence against the servant did not come from God but from human beings, from themselves (Isa. 53.5–7). Their eyes – like the eyes of Job's so-called friends – were initially blinded by the old sacral theology according to which any violence against a victim which falls outside the public order is divine violence. After their conversion, however, they recognize that things are quite different. They were projecting their own sin on to God and saw a divine violence where only they and others were at work with their aggression. For them, conversion was not merely an ethical matter but led them to change their whole world-view.

Jesus suffered a fate which has surprising parallels with that of the chosen and smitten Servant. Like that Servant, first of all for him his ear, indeed his whole consciousness, was opened anew; he felt the aura of the divine breath and heard words of love which addressed him as son (Mark 1.9–11). Thanks to this experience he became capable of healing and liberating people who had been imprisoned by violent powers (Mark 5.1–17; 9.14–29). He proclaimed the nearness of a God who forgives his enemies, the sinners, by loving them first, and invites them to a shared meal. In accordance with this divine offer he calls on his hearers, too, to respond to evil with good: to love their enemies and do good to them, just as God makes his sun rise on the good and the evil (Matt. 5.43–48). They are to neutralize and overcome all approaches to evil by surprising actions: 'But if anyone strikes you on the right cheek, turn to him the other also; and if anyone would sue you and take your coat, let him have your cloak as well' (Matt. 5.39). Where such behaviour is extended, violence will be overcome at its roots, and a community of peace and justice, the kingdom of God on earth, will begin to blossom.

However, despite its liberating and healing power, the activity of Jesus provoked resistance. First of all his opponents sought to lay traps for him (the question of tax, the adulterous woman, and so on). Still, with his creative imagination Jesus found surprising ways out of critical situations, and he was able to make the dangerous questions addressed to him rebound on his enemies in the form of admonitions ('Render to Caesar that which is Caesar's, and to God that which is God's.' 'Let him among you who is without sin cast the first stone.'). Nevertheless, Jesus' superior and creative reactions hardened the resistance, and this led him to respond to his opponents with a challenging proclamation of judgment. He showed how deep the powers of falsehood and violence go in people and demonstrated their ultimate consequences. But in so doing at the same time he made his own proclamation ambiguous. Was his message of the prior good just one side of a twofold image of God, as some images in his parables of judgment suggest, or did he understand judgment in quite a different way, as many subtle details suggest, namely as the disclosure of the process by which people judge one another and so continue the spiral of violence endlessly?

The proclamation of judgment did not bear the desired fruit, since it did not stir people up but gave the conflict a final twist. It provoked Jesus' opponents to open violence and thus compelled Jesus himself to adopt a decisive standpoint: would he call on God to punish his enemies by force or would he follow the course that he had proclaimed to the end? He gave his answer less by words than by his actions. He did not resort to counter-violence, nor did he beg for divine vengeance, as Jeremiah had done in a similar situation (Jer. 15.15). In prayer to God and in struggling with the anguish of his own death he radicalized his message of the priority of good so that it became the practice of unconditional non-violence: on the cross he prayed for his enemies and thus transformed the deadly aggression which struck him into loving surrender. In so doing he transformed all the archaic notions of sacrifice into a sacrifice of a totally new kind. He could act in this way because God had awoken his ear anew every day and because he had been allowed to experience that as the lord of life and death this God can raise new life.

To 'sacrifice' one's life in fighting and hatred against enemies does not ask too much of human forces, as the many wars in history show. But have we human beings the strength to take the way of love to the end in the face of direct violence? The disciples of Jesus attempted this and at first failed. Despite their closeness to their master, there was much about him that they did not understand, and at the critical moment they were carried along by fear of their fellow human beings. The world of anxiety and the infectious mechanisms of violence were stronger than their good will and drove them to betrayal. The completely different behaviour of their master asked to much of them, but at the same time led them to shed bitter tears (cf. Matt. 26.75). They were freed from this distress and desperation by the appearances of the risen Christ. The peace of Easter and thus forgiveness for their lack of faith was promised to the very people who had failed.[4]

The God who reveals himself in the dramatic fate of Jesus and his disciples thus shows himself to the end as a God who responds to evil with good. Even in the face of deadly violence he inspired Jesus to non-violence, and in the face of open betrayal he gave the disciples the word of forgiveness and peace through the risen Christ. At the same time this makes it clear that the overcoming of violence does not lie in the autonomous power of human beings. Jesus could go his way only by listening day by day to the word of his heavenly Father, and his disciples were made to see how the threat of violence and anxiety was stronger than their good will and how only the divine forgiveness had opened up a future for them. From the Christian perspective there is therefore no ethic of overcoming violence which could address an autonomous subject. Only in the light and in the power of the spirit of Pentecost, which is to open our ears and hearts every day, can we attempt to overcome the destructive powers. Here we have to be guided by both the way of Jesus and the experience of the disciples. Both ways together – the example of Jesus and the picture of our weaknesses – can show us how in the power of the divine spirit the abysmal world of violence with its power, which is not only terrifying but also fascinating and overwhelming, can step by step be illuminated and overcome. For this we need a way in the community of those who pursue a similar goal and by whose love and forgiveness we, too, can have a concrete experience of the divine love. Whether this love and the spirit of Pentecost are in fact effective in a community can be seen from whether people are gathered and united through forgiveness and repentance and no longer through polarization on enemies. If this happens, then at the same time those dark powers of collective violence are disclosed which had been hidden under a sacral veil since the beginning of humankind (cf. Matt. 13.35),[5] and had made groups capable of survival only through polarization against common foes.

4. An ethic for reducing violence?

If according to the Christian view violence can be overcome only under the guidance of the divine spirit in a community of fellow believers, then the further question arises whether there can be at least a universal ethic of the reduction of violence in the public and political sphere. A look at history can pave the way for an answer.

Jesus never claimed political power, and he seems to have taken it for granted that rulers oppress their people and that the powerful misuse their power (Matt. 20.25). According to the Gospel of John he explained to Pilate how the kingdom that he wanted to establish was of quite a different nature above all by saying that he had no servants to fight for him (John 18.36). But at the same time he acknowledged that Pilate had his power from above.

The community after Easter at first continued to follow this course. It kept away from political power but recognized that the state authority was in the service of God (Rom. 13.1–7) – though in quite a different way from the community of believers. Because of this only very indirect service, it initially did not develop any special political programme for the state and the improvement of the world, but expected that the violence of this world would soon pass away (I Cor. 7.31). Nevertheless, with its proclamation it made a public claim and thus came into conflict with the political authority. In this crisis many believers showed that, like Jesus, in trust in God they were ready and able to follow the way of non-violence to the end as martyrs.

But the public claim also prepared the church gradually to adopt its own public responsibility. Therefore the shift under Constantine did not bring about a break, though it did change the accents markedly. Since Christians in political offices now had themselves to use violence to maintain public order, and since the distinction between church and state was for long not seen clearly enough, though it was always emphasized, new ideas rapidly came to the fore which were in fact the old ones. A political theology arose from Old Testament texts about the judgment and wrath of God, from New Testament images of judgment which were understood apart from the way of Jesus, and from the political need to use violence. In this theology, the internal dynamic of the way of Jesus was heavily covered over and concealed by old sacral conceptions. Once again the ethical and political distinction between legitimate and illegitimate violence took on central significance; here the direct interests of the church often helped to define what was legitimate and what was not. It is hard to assess whether in this way there was a real reduction of violence in the history of Christianity or whether the mixture of church and state interest did not have the opposite effect; the question can be left open here.

The modern critical assessment of violence came about above all through this problem of what is legitimate and what is not. The wars of religion already showed how this judgment largely depended on one's own prejudice, and other wars between Christian nations pointed in the same direction. The modern development of armaments further led to a new experience, of how devastating and destructive even the so-called just use of force can be. That raised in a new form the question whether destructive violence cannot be overcome in principle.

In his work *On Eternal Peace* (1795), in view of the escalation of violence in the French Revolution Kant relied above all on the spirit of trade to achieve more peace between individuals and peoples. In so doing he was taking up a notion which had already interested the Scottish moralists and founders of political economics (Adam Smith, etc.). The world-wide market could in fact play an important role in the question of violence. Inspired by Girard's theory, P. Dumouchel and J.-P. Dupuy have demonstrated a clear connection between the sacral containment of violence in pre-state societies and the containment of violence through the market economy in the modern inter-state world.[6] Just as the sacral stems from the collective and yet stands over against it as a pre-existing power, so prices arise from interactions in the market economy and pre-exist individual partners in such a way that they dictate decisions and thus can prevent violent conflicts. Just as the sacral regularly needs its victims, so the modern market also produces its victims, though these are disguised in a new way. Whereas in the archaic world the initially profane victim was sacralized, the modern market economy gives the appearance of not being responsible for the many victims. But in both cases we have a system which creates victims and at the same time limits violence: the market restrains violence. That this comparison between the modern market economy and the old sacral world touches on a decisive point is also evident from the tendency towards the mythological in the modern media, which essentially belong to the world of the market. In a new edition of McLuhan's *Understanding Media*, L. Lapham writes: 'The postmodern imagination is a product of the mass media, but as a means of perception it is more accurately described as pre-Christian . . . As McLuhan noticed thirty years ago, the accelerated technologies of the electronic future carry us backward into the firelight flickering in the caves of a neolithic past.'[7] Advertising, which increasingly takes on features of sacral rituals, also belongs in this world which is at the same time both modern and neolithic.

What pre-state societies and the modern international world have in common is that neither knows a central authority which could shape public life on the basis of a deliberate decision. Processes of self-organization which involve violence create order by both containing violence and disguising its activity. In these worlds there is no independent and systematic place for a political ethic. Only that minimal ethic is called for which is necessary for the functioning of the system as a whole. At most there is a place for conscious ethical efforts to reduce violence in those niches which are not directly exposed to the pressure of international mechanisms.

The situation would be different, and ethical decisions for a comprehensive reduction of violence would again be possible, if there was an international authority which could dictate decisions both to the worldwide market and to regional parties in conflict. So an ethic of the reduction of violence must work for a world authority with a monopoly of violence. However, not only are the traditions of the many cultures against this but above all also the very real fear that in our one world there would be less open but far more structural violence.

Consequently the ethic of the reduction of violence faces the decisive question whether this risk is to be taken. The answer to this question transcends any ethic and again leads to the centre of religion. The risky decision about a whole world order can be taken only on the basis of a whole world-view. From a Christian perspective there are many reasons for thinking the risk worth taking.[8] For faith it is clear that our world will never be perfect, and the community of faith may also be sufficiently certain that it can offer resistance to the open or subtle pressure of totalitarian ideologies even in a world which is politically more uniform, and that its own manner of the overcoming of violence in faith will always have an effect on the public in one way or another. But there is no certainty in these questions relating to the future. Consequently the problem of violence makes it particularly clear that humanity never has its own fate in its hands. It is delivered over to powers which derive to a great degree from itself but by which at the same time it is asked too much. Only in trust in the one God who still embraces a destiny that we cannot master can we ultimately look serenely at all the threats of violence.

Translated by John Bowden

Notes

1. Cf. E. L Tuveson, *Redeemer Nation. The Idea of America's Millennial Role*, Chicago 1968.
2. C. Meier, *Die Entstehung des Politischen bei den Griechen*, Frankfurt 1980, 208.
3. R. Girard, *Violence and the Sacred*, Baltimore 1977.
4. For more detail see R. Schwager, *Jesus im Heilsdrama. Entwurf einer biblischen Erlösungslehre*, Innsbruck ²1996.
5. R. Girard, *Things Hidden since the Foundation of the World: Research Undertaken in Collaboration with Jean-Michel Oughourlian and Guy Lefort*, London and Stanford, Ca. 1987.
6. P. Dumouchel and J.-P. Dupuy, *L'enfer des choses. René Girard et la logique de l'économie*, Paris 1979.
7. L. Lapham, Introduction to M. McLuhan, *Understanding Media. The Extension of Man*, Cambridge, Mass. 1994, XIXf.
8. Vgl. H. Buchele, *Eine Welt oder keine Welt. Sozialethische Grundfragen angesichts einer ausbleibenden Weltordnungspolitik*, Innsbruck 1996.

Documentation: Religion and Violence

Edward Schillebeeckx

In its modern and postmodern version, and even perhaps beyond all postmodernity, our Western world is in search of new sense of what used to be called human destiny. However, some postmoderns believe that such questions about meaning are not 'meaningful'. On the one hand our contemporaries want to escape a terrorizing dogmatism of individuals, systems and religions which believe that they have a monopoly of all truth and therefore in the course of history as we know it marginalize, suspect and mercilessly exclude all those who think otherwise. On the other hand, most want to escape a radical relativism which knows neither norms nor values, neither loyalty nor free ties, and in this way makes human dignity problematic. This can happen in a condescending or merciless way, depending on the circumstances, de-humanizing humanity so that it becomes at any rate a bizarre and often a playful something, a game and/or a holocaust!

We can see religion in its concrete manifestations as a cultural form of salvation from God. Ideological misunderstanding and ideological misuse are then just round the corner. Human beings are the subjects of religion, but these human subjects are also cultural beings. Therefore the specific culture in which believers live is that on which, for example, Christian faith is really modelled; at the same time it is that through which this faith is assimilated on a living way; and finally it is that in which faith is practised concretely by people living here and now. Because religion is mediated through society and culture, when there are fundamental shifts in the cultural pattern of society and in the categories of thought and experience current in that society, believers find it hard to deal with the pre-existing cultural forms of traditional faith. Moreover, as a result of these changes religion can associate itself with aspects of violence in the given culture and then can itself also become violent as religion, since sociologically it is an element in society. Furthermore, when they consider the actual historical violence in many religions, Christianity by no means excepted, and take into account the wars of religion which are still raging to the present day, some people are even asking whether the religious reference to the Absolute is not *per se* experienced as violent, above all in a so-called 'postmodern age', and is not therefore fundamentally disqualified.

The fact that religion, as the concrete form of our relationship to the Absolute/Transcendent which is at the same time the Absolute/Immanent, is itself an element of cultures warns us to be extremely careful. If culture both in its 'horizontal' and also in its 'vertical' (or 'depth') dimension of self-transcendence is a movement in history which pushes back frontiers, on the empirical level we are confronted directly with the phenomenon of violence. That, moreover, is often the objection of many people when the term 'transcendence' (or the Absolute and Ultimate) is introduced into a discussion of our earthly culture. And a look at our human history confirms this objection in a shattering way.

The sense of superiority which religions, certainly not excluding Christianity, have in fact repeatedly shown proves to be one of the greatest obstacles to the human cohabitation of different religions within the same state frontiers, as is increasingly the case in our day: thus for example in some countries Muslims and Buddhists are neighbours of Christians, whom they meet every day. Any sense of superiority threatens a worthwhile culture. So we must come clean over the history of the encounters between religions (in reality, between religious people), a history which displays so much violence unworthy of human beings for an ideal or a great cause, for what is claimed to be the sole truth, or for a particular religious relationship to the Absolute.

If we want to grasp this historical reality, the question becomes pressing whether there is an intrinsic connection between religion by its very nature, i.e. its relationship to the transcendent-immanent Absolute, and religious violence. If this is not the case (and that is my thesis), then the real history of the encounter of religions automatically raises a second question: is not religion in its assertion of truth in practice tied up with various presuppositions which are alien to religion, or perceived to be stuck in a particular unhealthy and unjustified self-understanding? Such an entanglement can mean a betrayal of the deepest dynamic of any relationship to the Absolute, including the specifically Christian or authentic gospel relationship, and the religious relationship becomes violent precisely because of this entanglement.

Within this group of problems history finally raises a third question, namely the tricky question of the historical claim of Israel or the church to 'election' and a covenant with God: 'God is with us.'

When we read in the Sermon on the Mount, 'You are blessed if you are meek and act justly', we ask how it is possible for the history of Christianity to have been so heavily distorted by religious violence, all the more so since as Christians we worship the living God who, we confess, wills to be a God of human beings, not of the dead but of the living, a God whom already the 'fathers of faith' in their Jewish roots confessed to be a God 'for whom human sacrifices are an abomination' (Lev. 18.21–30; 20.1–5).

Before I analyse the complex of this threefold problem, I want to say that this actual contradiction between the behaviour of religious people and their relationship to the Absolute is all too human and to some degree understandable. If religion is the most significant value in human life, as people who believe in God experience it to be and may rightly claim it to be, then any theoretical or practical misuse of religion leads to the cruellest inhumanities. Here too the corruption of the best is the worst. People have fought and killed in the course of history in the name of God. People today who are attempting to rationalize this problem after countless wars of religion often find it difficult to sort out in an understandable way. They then often come to the conclusion, albeit wrongly, that there must be an intrinsic connection between religion and violence. I say that this is wrong. But on the other hand we certainly cannot just discuss away the actual relationship between religion and violence by trivializing this historical connection and attributing it to the weakness and inconsistency of believers. The perplexing fact that great theologians who were even meek by nature, including Thomas Aquinas, as children of their time legitimated violence theologically, indicates that the matter is not so simple, above all for people who experience their relationship to the Absolute or ineffable Mystery as the core of their existence, as a question of life and death.

Here I shall not go further into a thesis like that of e.g. Merleau-Ponty, who claims that religious violence is intrinsic to the nature of religion (though it is worth remembering). For this form of atheism the reference to the Absolute means the death of all that is relative and contingent, and also the death of human autonomy. This position is outmoded today even for many agnostics and above all humanists. It does not always distort the practice of most religions, but it does distort their soul. Thomas Aquinas expresses this powerfully in his doctrine of creation. This issues in the fact that the act of creation places human beings in their autonomous, albeit finite and mortal, humanity and gives them free responsibility for their ethical action in the world and for the autonomous quest for ethical criteria for their action. God establishes human beings in their own human and self-conscious rights; anyone who shakes these, says

Thomas, shakes God himself. Anyone who gets too close to human beings has to deal with God.

Thus in principle, rightly, any religion is subject to the critique of 'human dignity' both on a human and also on a Christian basis. The authentic relationship to the Absolute as such is in no respect violent; quite the opposite. It generates undeterred courage to realize more humanity in all spheres of life.

But the difficulty is that this relationship to the Absolute is never given in a 'detached' way: for believers nothing can escape this bond of creation with the Absolute in the human sphere. From our perspective this immediate link between God and us is always mediated. And of course that opens up the possibility of all kinds of good, but also false, associations between religious people and 'worldly' intermediaries, if these intermediaries are elevated above their own status and directly promoted without further ado to the status of the will of God. For in that case false alliances can spur on religious people to religious violence in the name of their relationship to the Absolute.

The question is whether a claimed relationship to the Absolute, to the Transcendent or to the Mystery liberates human beings or threatens them. From a human and Christian perspective, is violence in the name of religion essentially from the evil one? My firm view is that it is, and I shall demonstrate that.

Religious violence (and thus of course also the repudiation of inter-religious dialogue on the basis of equal rights) has a twofold foundation of a non-religious and also non-Christian kind. In other words, these foundations are false.

1. The first false foundation is the claim of a religion to be the only true religion

Here the right of other religions to exist is consistently denied. In a multicoloured society such a negation is in itself a virtual declaration of war and thus amounts to violence. Religion, including Christianity, comes under the criticism of a hermeneutic or clarification of existence which 'makes people experience justice' simply on grounds of humanity; for believers, moreover, this is on the Christian and religious grounds of belief in creation. However, these two grounds cannot be put together as two parts. Humanity, human dignity, is the direct basis for a human ethic (*Ac si*, i.e. as if – I am not saying *etsi* although – *Deus non daretur*, God did not exist), and on this direct human basis according to Christian faith God's creation is the absolute or religious ground which cannot be added to the *humanum* because it is transcendent/immanent.

It follows from this structure that traces of this religious transcendence can be found in the sphere of the autonomous realm of humanity, especially if observers set what seems to them here and now to be ethically worthy of human beings against the light of a given religious tradition of experience, which for Christians is the Jewish-Christian tradition. There can be no question of a direct transparency: only in the light of a religious tradition of humanity can the redundancy of a religious transcendence in the ethical and human sphere really be perceived.

That brings us to the second problem. Even if our own religion is not regarded as the only true religion, a second religious claim means that religions are in fact violent.

2. Religion established as the direct guarantee of the well-being of human society

This second foundation for religious violence is the conviction of some religious people that their own religion is their first civic duty, on the basis of its claim that the God whom they confess is the direct guarantee of the well-being of human society. Even though such a view does not make any claim to the sole absoluteness of the religion of its adherents it similarly leads to religious violence. Even if a religion recognizes itself as one alongside many other religions, it can incite violence because of all kinds of alliances or presuppositions, hidden or open, which are in fact bound up with it and therefore because of an implied distorted picture of God.

History gives us countless arguments in support of this. It already emerges from the ancient concept of *religio* which was established in Roman law. There religion was the first and supreme national duty of citizens, *pietas*, and any deviation from it was said to be a danger to the state and was therefore heavily punished, even though in the Hellenistic-Roman pantheon there was room for many kinds of gods. Despite this tolerant pantheon, the first Christians were persecuted because from the perspective of this Latin-Hellenistic law they were atheists. In other words they were persecuted for their denial of the divine guarantee of the well-being of the Roman empire and because as a result they were failing in their duty to the state and were seen as a danger to it. If we remember how in this Roman law *religio* was the first civic duty, a direct link between the established or – as an alternative – the *per se* revolutionary social and political society and the relationship to the Absolute as a guarantee of this established (or revolutionary) reason of state, then violence between religions and thus against human beings is a logical and consistent outcome. Here people were not even aware that such religious violence was 'inhuman', since according to that view, outside this relationship to the Absolute, human beings were entangled even worse in various kinds of slavery or violence.

Now when in the fourth century Christianity became a state religion, the church took over the Roman concept of *religio* (and the concept of 'Roma' bound up with it) and transferred it to the Christian relation to the Absolute. So from now on (in the West for centuries) the God of the Christians became the guarantor of the actual established political order of the state, with all the consequences which followed for those who were regarded as deviants, as 'heretics' or 'schismatics'. From this perspective 'thinking otherwise' was simply regarded as *lèse majesté*. That made possible the punishment of 'heretical Christians' by the civic authorities. Thus, for example, reasons of state stood one hundred per cent behind the council which condemned Arius, because for the emperor the anti-Arian dogma was the strongest weapon in his effort to unite the empire. Arianism thus became a danger to the state. The church's adoption of the ancient Roman concept of *religio* later made possible the Crusades in which Muslim were mown down, and also the Inquisition by which deviants from the true faith, a danger to the well-being of the state, were handed over to the civil power as a danger to the state and sent to the stake.

In such a case religious violence does not (or does not *per se*) rest on the claim of a religion to be the only true religion, but on a false and ideological, uncritical assumption that the religious relationship to the Absolute implies a direct connection with the concrete social and political order created by human beings, to which people belong, in other words to the assumption that for example the God of Christians is the direct guarantor of the social and political order or what is proclaimed as a natural ethic and is thus the well-being of the kingdom (*salus nationis* as *lex suprema*, directly guaranteed by God). And the other side of the coin is that to be a non-Christian was regarded as potentially and even virtually dangerous to the state. Even tolerant modern states ultimately take violent action against elements and activities which are a danger to the state. It is not the Christian religion as such, but its alliance with the ancient concept of *religio* and the direct elevation of a pretended morality to the will of God, which explains the religious violence of Christianity in history. That is also the explanation of the historical fact that even critical theologians have in their time found it quite easy to provide theological legitimation for this religious violence.

What follows from this theologically for us today is crystal clear. We cannot accept the assumption that the relation to the Absolute has a direct connection with the preservation of an established order or (as an actual but rarer alternative) with a direct religious call to revolution. In other words, to make a direct connection between the Absolute and a particular social and political order on earth (whether 'established' or 'revolutionary') by nature amounts to a misuse of religion and is therefore to be rejected on grounds of both humanity and Christianity. Therefore in my view a 'state religion', too, as a reality is essentially threatening to human beings and potentially violent. That applies equally to the state recognition of some preferred 'official religions', excluding or merely tolerating others (though here, too, the urgent question remains how far concrete religions are liberating or threatening to human beings in their relationship to what they call the Absolute).

Still quite apart from theological and biblical arguments, simply for humane and ethical reasons it is reprehensible and discriminating to claim that there is a direct connection between a particular religion and a concrete social and political order. In essence such a statement already implies a violation of human rights and thus, in religious language, of rights on the basis of God's creation. Anyone who comes too close to human beings has to deal with God! In a pluralist society this amounts to a virtual declaration of war on others, in other words violence. That is by no means to deny that the gospel is relevant to politics and society; it is simply to say that there is no direct intrinsic connection between the Christian confession of God and the social and political order that we have realized or seek to realize. Moreover, the very repudiation of any direct connection of this kind gives Christians space for an inter-religious dialogue on the basis of equality between all dialogue partners, despite the actual religious differences. This does not, however, mean that all religions are 'equal', the view of so-called indifferentism.

In reality the Christian denial of these two distorted forms of religious self-understanding is establishing itself only slowly, and above all only under social pressure from outside, namely from the modern secularized world. This is an 'alien prophecy' from which even Christian churches can learn a lot. Yet such pressure is itself already a gain, though it is also necessary to look further for intrinsic religious and Christian grounds for a non-violent religion and for an open inter-religious dialogue, and for a specifically Christian positive attitude to men and women of other religious orientations.

3. Divine covenant and election

I am certainly aware that the previous discussion raises a critical question about our traditional interpretation of Christianity's so-called claim to absoluteness and the use of terms like election and divine covenant in Judaism, Christianity and Islam. I can see that this will have to lead us to the conviction that while the notion of election by God in fact includes mediation, it does not involve any partisanship which threatens human beings, and thus can only envisage universality, and not exclusion. That means that election and covenant are subordinate to the creative intention of God, who wills the salvation of all men and women: the whole of humankind is the elect people of God. All historical forms of belief in a religious election must be at the service of and subject to the criticism of universal election; otherwise the self-understanding of election in individuals, peoples, or faith communities also poses a threat, involves danger and violence, to those of other faiths or none at all. This can prove a breeding ground of violence.

The discussion of these three points may perhaps confuse some Christians. Do not my assertions endanger the legitimate content of the Christian claim to the uniqueness of Jesus Christ?

I cannot analyse this problem fully here, but I do not want simply to pass over it in silence.

My thesis is that in its distinctive nature Christianity is essentially bound up with an unsurpassable 'historical peculiarity' and thus is limited. It is not a question of denying or minimizing the eschatological character of Jesus whom we confess as Christ, but of eliminating the Christian claim to absolute truth, as it has been concentrated over the course of time in a network of imperialistic features, whether in an exclusivist or an inclusivist sense.

On the one hand we may not avoid the question of truth about the character of religions; on the other hand, any believer (of whatever religion) must avoid both an absolutism and a relativism. The relationship between the religions must be resolved in a way which entails no discrimination against other religions and does not reflect a sense of its own superiority. But we may not and need not surrender our own deepest convictions to the liberalism which simply sees the many world religions meeting different needs on the market.

Religions all have their own identities, and in character are all unique by comparison with the other religions. Within this context, the special feature of Christianity lies in the fact that in the Christian view a historical and thus limited, finite peculiarity of the human being Jesus of Nazareth reveals the life and nature of God as salvation of human beings. The difficulty is not that Jesus is unique and at the same time historically contingent; most religions know comparable descriptions. The difficulty is that it is of the essence of the Christian claim that God's final or eschatological form of revelation which brings salvation is communicated through Jesus, the Christ. That is the core of the whole of the New

Testament and the Christian tradition of experience which emerged from him.

The key question is whether this basic confession, of the New Testament and Christianity generally, does not already discriminate against other religions, which as a result are devalued, so that their self-undertanding is misunderstood, or whether it bears a message that is liberating for all men and women.

A misunderstanding of this basic Christian confession is possible in two directions. On the one hand one can overlook the concrete, special humanity of Jesus precisely as a human being: as a human being Jesus is shaped by a particular region and culture, and has a specific geographical situation which limits him. If we overlook this we make the human being Jesus a necessary 'divine emanation', as a result of which all other religions fade away to nothing. In a docetic way this theological position degrades Jesus' real humanity so that it becomes a historical pseudo-reality. On the other hand Christians cannot overlook the definitive or eschatological character of what happened in Jesus Christ, which they confess. This confession, and not all kinds of other church doctrines or church laws, whether inclusive or non-inclusive, decides whether they are Christians. Clearly we must be very careful about these problems, and use sensitive formulations. For in Christian theology one cannot absolutize a single special historical phenomenon specifically in its historicity. That is even the case with the historical humanity of Jesus of Nazareth. Otherwise we find ourselves contradicting the Christian belief in creation. God as transcendent is in no respect whatsoever an element in an earthly system or a human social and political order, nor is God the 'ingredient' of a religion. However, this de-transcending of God or encapsulation of God even in a religious system has not only taken place often in the past, but still continues to leave its mark today, above all in the casual false application of the theory of the *communicatio idiomatum*, in which properties of God are simply transferred to the human being Jesus. Moreover, this offends against the Council of Chalcedon. As Christians we may never forget that neither Christianity nor even the human being Jesus is absolute, or absolutely one or unique; that can be said only of the God of Jesus, the creator, the God of all human beings. According to Christian faith in Jesus, the Absolute – which means God – is reflected in historical form and thus in historical relativity. For Christians, Jesus is a relative (because historical) manifestation of a meaning which is, however, absolute.

That the character and identity of Jesus take form in historical particularity means that the distinctions between the individual world religions are better left in their authentic singularity and uniqueness and not done away with. There is therefore also more truth in all the religions together than in one particular religion, Christianity not excepted. In God's absolutely free divinity God is so 'over-defined' that God's fullness cannot be exhausted by a particular, historically limited religion or tradition of religious experience.

Granted, Christians confess that 'the fullness of God dwells bodily in Jesus', but this dwelling takes place precisely in the humanity of Jesus and thus in a limited, unavoidably alienating and refractory prism. It is an expression of contingency, and thus the limited form of this appearing of God's fullness in our precarious history. Therefore there are true, good and beautiful – surprising – positive and irreducible aspects in the many forms of religious understanding of God, including forms which have found and find no place in the specific experience of Christianity. There are differences in the experience of the relationship with God which cannot be swept away. Furthermore there are various authentic religious practices which Christians have adopted or practised and perhaps, because of the particular emphases placed by Jesus, cannot adopt without doing violence to these particular emphases, since to do so would force them to the periphery and rob Jesus of his particular prophetic sharpness. It is that sharpness which ultimately shapes their specific and prophetic Christianity. The multiplicity of religions is not an evil which must be removed at all costs. However, the mutual quarrels and wars of religion must be done away with. The religions can expect to be enriched by one another only in so far as this is compatible with their own authentic religious accents.

Here I am not denying that the historical multiplicity of religion, which cannot be done away with in principle, is inwardly nourished and supported by an implicit unity. This unity cannot be thematized as such in our history, but it is nevertheless real: it is the unity of the one God, which is the concern of religions. This implicit transcendent unity is reflected in the historically immanent family similarities between the religions, and that justifies us in giving all these different religious configurations the single name 'religion'. The character and identiy of Christianity – the essential coupling of the final or eschatological coming of the kingdom of God with the historical person of Jesus of Nazareth – is at the same time its unavoidable historical contingency and thus a finite limitation.

Christians can find it difficult to adopt this notion, this insight of faith. Many think that it goes too far. Others think that such a view still does not go far enough and detach (usually tacitly) the historical figure of Jesus from the content of the confession which accompanies it, the Christ. But in the history of faith Jesus makes no sense without 'Christ', and conversely the confession of Christ does not make any sense without the historical Jesus. Without the historical figure of Jesus and without the Christian 'church confession', which appears in the same human history, that he is the

Christ, the Son of God (a confession which is based on the manifold dealings of the disciples with this historical figure), today we would not know a Jesus of Nazareth. Far less would he be the source of inspiration for our own personal, interpersonal and political lives and at the same time the offer of a real religious possibility of life for others. Only in this way do we avoid the exclusivist ideology of election. Otherwise election *per se* includes discrimination and virtual imperialism, and thus also violence. Jesus' election is regarded as a mediation towards universality; it is at the service of all men and women without exception, and therefore is not threatening to human beings but liberating even for those who are 'not preferred'. With good reason I put as an introductory motto to my book *Church* the vigorous prophetic accusation of the prophet Amos to his people Israel: 'As I brought Israel out of Egypt, so I brought the Philistines from Caphtor, and Aram from Kir' (Amos 9.7). At that time Israel believed that it could escape God's judgment because it knew itself to be the elect people. Amos by no means denies this election, but for him election always means the service of all humankind. Personal election is at the service of universality, which has priority over election and thus relativizes it. In other words, the personal is put into a relationship of service with the concrete and universal: the salvation of all human beings without any partisanship to threatens anyone. So election in no way means a preferential position from which one can do great things (Amos 6.1).

Now the Christian confession that the historical Jesus is the Lord, the glorified Christ, corresponds to and breaks with that notion of partisan election to the disadvantage of others. However, in that case one must take seriously the special significance of the death of Jesus and his resurrection from death as the act of God. Precisely in the 'historical failure' which has become manifest in the execution of Jesus, the ideology of a direct connection between God and any concrete historical phenomenon, even though this be the human being Jesus, is abolished. For in his death Jesus remains a contingent finite being belonging to God's covenant with Israel. As such this particular death cannot produce any direct connection with God the Absolute, nor can it be salvation of the whole of humankind through a purely forensic election. Jesus himself indeed said that he had come only for the twelve tribes of Israel; we cannot sweep away this reality. In Jesus, whom we confess as the Christ, something else must therefore have been at work. How else can we understand the whole judgment pericope in the Gospel of Matthew, in which the 'relation to the other' is decisive for the salvation of each individual (Matt. 25.31–46)? 'What you have done to the least of these little ones' (and Jesus identifies himself with these little ones) is finally decisive for life and death. The affirmation or repudiation of the other in his or her situation of otherness and as an alien, even outside every conscious relationship to Jesus Christ and even to God, is decisive for the salvation of the Jew, the Christian, the humanist or whomever.

But there is a problem here! Is not the making of a direct connection between the 'innocent death' of Jesus and the relationship to the Absolute not itself an ideology which threatens human beings? Certainly I used to assume that the grain of truth in the statement 'redeemed by Jesus despite his death' had to lie somehow in what I had called the 'historical fiasco on the cross'. For after the death of Jesus the history of disaster and violence simply keeps following its old course, as though there had been no messiah. There is little of redemption and liberation to be seen in the world. On earth and in our history there will obviously never be a paradise or a saving state, not even for those who believe in Jesus Christ.

However, now I am beginning gradually to realize the consequences of my remark about the historical fiasco of Jesus' death. On the cross there is a man who is suffering a defeat in his radical commitment to a good cause. For this fiasco includes the fact that even in Jesus there is a radical challenging of any direct saving connection between a concrete historical event (even the death of Jesus) and a relation to the Absolute. On the cross, Jesus' relation to the Absolute melted away into a dark night: 'My God, why have you forsaken me?' (Mark 15.34). Is there then a direct relationship to the Absolute 'despite' Jesus' death, thanks to his trusting faith: 'Father, into your hands I commend my spirit' (Luke 23.46)?

Thus it becomes clear that the place preferred (by God) for encounter with God is the face of the suffering human being, the place of the *Jesus crucifixus*. The crucifixion of Jesus is about Jesus' experience of the silent presence of the gracious God. It is about the trust of a human being in God in extreme helplessness. His God is silent. Here it becomes clear that no single historical contingent given can ever have a sacral or absolute value to which human beings could cling as a secure foundation for happiness and well-being on earth, as individuals or as a society.

Even *the* elect, Jesus of Nazareth, does not receive a single guarantee for any earthly or historical resting place. He is directed towards the silent transcendent God who in Jesus makes himself the 'brother' of suffering human beings threatened by violence.

Thus there is a direct connection between the earthly event of a 'dark night' and Jesus' inner relationship to the Absolute. But that means that the 'direct' positive relationship of the Absolute to our history is brought about where this history stops: at death, at the end of each personal history. In dying Jesus refused to repay violence with violence. He forgives those who kill him violently. The liberating moment does not lie in death as such, but in the reality that this death is taken up into the silent presence of

God in an act of forgiveness based on the trust of faith. It is taken into the silent presence of the one who elevates Jesus to being the heavenly messiah who from now on can give to all the Holy Spirit who is not bound to anything, a spirit of reconciliation. For the incarnation is not just an event in time; while it indeed began with the conception of Jesus, it continued through his whole life and came to completion in Jesus' exalted life with God.

Paul perhaps quotes one of the earliest Christian confessions of faith: 'The gospel concerning his son, who was descended from David according to the flesh and designated Son of God in power according to the Spirit of holiness by his resurrection from the dead, Jesus Christ our Lord' (Rom. 1.3–4). In the event of the cross it proves that even the 'incarnation' (as the supreme form of election) of the Son of God as a historical phenomenon (Jesus of Nazareth) makes all election and every covenant subject to the universalist intention of creation: the salvation of all human beings. We sometimes forget that without the elevation or glorification of Jesus to be Christ and Lord his death would in fact have been 'in vain', as Paul says. The Gospel of John really says the same thing: 'It is good for you that I go away, otherwise the Holy Spirit cannot come' (John 16.7). God does not save his own from death. The filial relationship between Father and Son was no guarantee that the man Jesus, the elect, would be spared this shameful death. Even in Jesus there is no direct relationship between earthly happiness and well-being and his religious (filial) relationship to the Absolute. This is the absolute seriousness of the incarnation. That salvation from God runs counter to our whole earthly history means that God takes the helplessness of our human condition more seriously than we do. 'In Christ God was reconciling the world to himself, not counting their trespasses against them, and entrusting to us the message of reconciliation' (II Cor. 5.19). In the Gospel of John, moreover, the Easter event is related to the gift of reconciliation by the Spirit. This Spirit is not 'incarnate' in our contingent earthly history and therefore is not limited, but transcends it. Precisely because of this, however, as the spirit of God sent by the exalted Christ it blows in a life-giving way wherever human beings are to be found. Even after the first coming of Jesus no single sacral resting place can be found in our earthly history. Believers are directed to the silent presence of God, to forgiveness despite everything, to the incomprehensible free gift of the Spirit of God, which could only be given to all who are open to it after Jesus' death.

But precisely this spirit of God reminds us of the historical person Jesus. It reminds us of his prophetic message, his career and his death, freely accepted, as a protest against all violence. In his exaltation this historical figure is messiah for all men and women, thanks to Jesus' sending of the Holy Spirit.

Only in the Christian confession of the Holy Spirit (pneumatology) does christology come to its universal openness for all human beings without any discriminating undervaluing of all other religions. In the power of this gift of the Spirit, which is not bound to 'the church of Christ' – although thanks to precisely this Spirit the highly necessary memory of the man Jesus is kept alive in word and celebration – men and women can also forgive other and encounter 'the other' in his or her otherness and affirm that other. The actual historical violence of Christianity and its christology has its deepest roots in our continual forgetfulness of pneumatology. In it the redemption of Jesus becomes a historical and universal offer without any discrimination or virtual violence.

Only pneumatology can prevent christology, too, from being violent. Without pneumatology any christology is false in a way that threatens human beings and is unorthodox.

The actual historical violence of Christianity and its christology is most deeply rooted in our constant forgetfulness of pneumatology: the Logos of the pneuma blows where it wills.

Conclusion

This view has a certain affinity with the present discontent of many people with their own culture and their actual religion. Men and women long for a culture of justice and love. A culture of human rights is not enough, though it is a minimum and the beginning of love. But people long to be accepted unconditionally by others; each individual wants to be accepted for his or her own sake, whether they be black, yellow, cross-eyed, handicapped or alien. Respect, forgiveness, love and trust give people 'their due'. *Sui cuique bonum*! As a law, a 'right' is frosty and cold. A humane culture is ultimately a culture of love, and this cannot be laid down in laws or codified. Therefore a religious movement, a religion which is not inhumanely alienated from its own true roots, is one of the most dynamic forces in a human culture.

Without Christian humanity, Christianity will not be important in the future, but humanity will fall short of itself without a Christianity which is true to the gospel. In Christianity, as it is rooted in the gospel of Jesus as the Lord and coming Son of Man as judge of the world, there is an inexhaustible field of force also for cultural ethical human action with a view to more humanity for all.

Translated by John Bowden

Contributors

FRANÇOIS HOUTART was born in 1925, ordained priest in 1949, and gained his doctorate in sociology at the Catholic University of Louvain, of which he is professor emeritus. At present he is Director of the Tricontinental Centre at Louvain-la-Neuve and is editor of two journals, *Social Compass* and *Alternatives Sud*. He has written around fifty works on the sociology of religion, development and culture, including *The Church and Revolution* (1971), *Religion and Ideology in Sri Lanka* (1974), and *The Great Asiatic Religions and their Social Functions* (1981), and many articles on these topics.

Address: Centre Tricontinental, Avenue Sainte Gertrude 5, B 1348 Louvain-la-Neuve, Belgium.

PAUL NZACAHAYO was born in Rwanda in 1959 and educated there. Between 1980 and 1982 he was Secretary-Treasurer to the Legal Representative of the Free Methodist Church in Rwanda. He then became a pastor involved in church planning and development work in rural and remote areas, before being appointed Director of the Department of Evangelism in the Free Methodist Church of Rwanda in 1990 and in 1991 Director of that church's literacy programme. He gained an MTh and an MBA at New College, Edinburgh, where he is currently studying for a PhD.

Address: New College, Edinburgh University, Mound Place, Edinburgh EH1 2LX.

VIMAL TIRIMANNA was born in 1955 and after his college studies became a Redemptorist, being ordained priest in 1987. He gained his Licentiate and Doctorate in moral studies at the Alphonsian Academy in Rome, and since 1995 has been lecturer in moral theology at the National Seminary in Kandy, Sri Lanka. In 1996 he became Provincial Superior of the Redemptorist Fathers and Theological Consultant to the Federation of Asian Bishops' Conferences. Wildlife conservation has been a lifelong interest and he has written many articles on it for *LORIS*, the official journal of the Sri Lankan Wildlife and Nature Protection Society. He has also written many articles for *Vidyajyothi*, and 'Mass Media and its Effects on Just War Criteria in the Gulf War', *New Blackfriars*, April 1992.

Address: Frangipani Studentate, 80 Ampitiya Road, Kandy, Sri Lanka.

MIROSLAV VOLF is Associate Professor of Systematic Theology at Fuller Theological Seminary, Pasadena, California, and teaches Theology and Ethics at Evangelical Theological Faculty, Osijek, former Yugoslavia. He was born in Croatia in 1956 and studied theology and philosophy in his native country, in the United States and Germany. He holds a doctorate in theology from the Protestant Theological Faculty in Tübingen. He has published numerous scholarly articles, mainly on political and economic theology and ecclesiology. His books include *Work in the Spirit. Toward a Theology of Work*, New York 1991, and *Exclusion and Embrace: A Theological Exploration of Identity, Otherness and Reconciliation*, Nashville 1996. He is a member of the PC USA.

Address: Fuller Theological Seminary, School of Theology, 135 North Oakland Ave, Pasadena CA 91182, USA.

JON SOBRINO was born in the Basque Country in 1938 and educated in Spain, Germany and the USA. He became a Jesuit in 1956 and since 1957 has belonged to the Central American province of the Society, living mainly in El Salvador. He was ordained priest in 1969. He holds (unique among liberation theologians) a Master's Degree in engineering from St Louis University, and a doctorate in theology from the Hochschule Sankt Georgen in Frankfurt. He is the author of some twenty books, many of which have been translated into English, including *Christology at the Crossroads* (1976); *The True Church and the Poor* (1984); *Jesus in Latin America* (1986); *Spirituality of Liberation* (1988); *Companions of Jesus: The Murder and Martyrdom of the Salvadorean Jesuits* (1990); *Jesus the Liberator* (Vol. 1 of a projected two-volume christology, 1993). He is also joint editor with the late Ignacio Ellacuría of *Mysterium Liberationis: Fundamental Concepts of Liberation Theology* (1993).

Address: Mediterráneo 50, Jardines de la Guadalupe, San Salvador, El Salvador, CA.

HEDWIG MEYER-WILMES was born in 1953 in Harsewinkel, Germany; she studied Catholic theology, education and German in Münster and then worked as a teacher of religious education and an assistant in a parish, being involved in an emergency group for rape victims in Bielefeld. She became an assistant at the Catholic Ecumenical Institute in Münster; and then lecturer in feminist theology at the Catholic University of Nijmegen and a visiting professor in women's studies in Louvain. Her publications include *Rebellion auf der Grenze. Ortsbestimmung feministischer Theologie*, Freiburg, Basel and Vienna 1990; *Over hoeren, taarten en vrouwen, die voorbij gaan. Macht en verschil in de vrouwenkerk*, Kampen 1992 (with Lieve Troch); *Rebellion on the Borders. Feminist Theology between Theory and Praxis*, Kampen 1995; *Zwischen lila and lavendel. Schritte feministischer Theologie*, Regensburg 1996; *and Memoiren einer Schlange. Feministisch-theologische Gedichte* (forthcoming).

Address: Erasmusplein 1, NL 6525 HT Nijmegen, The Netherlands.

MARY GREY was born in the north of England in 1941 and studied Classics and Philosophy at Oxford, and then at the Catholic University of Louvain, Belgium. For five years she was Professor of Feminism and Christendom at the Catholic University of Nijmegen, the Netherlands, and is now Professor of Contemporary Theology at La Sainte Union College in the University of Southampton. She writes and lectures in Feminist Liberation Theology and coordinated the European delegation to the EATWOT dialogue of women theologians in Costa Rica in 1994, Women Struggling against Global Violence: A Spirituality for Life. She edits the journal *Ecotheology* – formerly *Theology in Green* – and among other publications has written *Redeeming the Dream*, London 1989, on redemption; *The Wisdom of Fools?*, London 1993, on revelation, and *Beyond the Dark Night – a Way forward for the Church?*, London 1997. She is currently engaged with ecclesiology from a feminist liberationist and ecological perspective. With her husband Nicholas Grey she set up a charity, Wells for India, and is involved in social work in Rajasthan.

Address; LSU College, University of Southampton, The Avenue, Southampton SO17 1EG.

ANDREA RICCARDI was born in Rome in 1950; he is now Professor of the History of Christianity at the University of Rome III. His particular interest is Christianity in the contemporary world, and especially its encounter with modernity. Recent books include *Pio XII*, Rome and Bari 1984; *Le chiese di Pio XII*, Rome and Bari 1986; *Il Vaticano e Mosca*, Rome and Bari 1993; *Il potere del Papa. Dal Pio XII a Giovanni Paolo II*, Rome and Bari 1993; *Il Mediterraneo nel Novecento*, Cinisello Balsamo 1994; *Intransigenza e modernitá. La Chiesa cattolica verso il terzo millennio*, Rome and Bari 1996.

Address: Comunità S. Egidio, Piazza E. Egidio 3/A, I 00153 Roma, Italy.

HERMANN HÄRING was born in 1937 and studied theology in Munich and Tübingen; between 1969 and 1980 he worked at the Institute of Ecumenical Research in Tübingen; since 1980 he has been Professor of Dogmatic

Theology at the Catholic University of Nijmegen. His books include *Kirche und Kerygma. Das Kirchenbild in der Bultmannschule*, 1972; *Die Macht des Bösen. Das Erbe Augustins*, 1979; *Zum Problem des Bosen in der Theologie*, 1985; he was a co-editor of the *Wörterbuch des Christentums*, 1988, and has written articles on ecclesiology and christology, notably in the *Tijdschrift voor Theologie*.

Address: Katholieke Universiteit, Faculteit der Godgeleerdheid, Erasmus-gebouw, Erasmusplein 1, 6525 HT Nijmegen, Netherlands.

JEAN PIERRE WILS was born in Geel, Belgium, in 1957. He studied philosophy and theology in Louvain and Tübingen and lectured on Christian ethics in Tübingen, gaining his doctorate in 1987 and his habilitation in 1991. Since 1996 he has been Professor of Moral Theology at the Catholic University of Nijmegen and is also a member of the governing body of the Centre for Ethics there. His publications include: *Sittlichkeit und Subjektivität* (1987); *Ästhetische Gute* (1991); *Die Grosse Erschöpfung* (1995), *Grundbegriffe der christlichen Ethik* (with D. Mieth, 1994) and numerous specialist articles on ethics and moral theology.

Address: Katholieke Universiteit, Faculteit der Godgeleerdheid, Erasmus-gebouw/Erasmusplein 1, 6525 HI Nijmegen, The Netherlands.

RAYMOND SCHWAGER SJ was born in Balterswil, Switzerland in 1935. Between 1970 and 1977 he was a member of the editorial board of the journal *Orientierung*; since 1977 he has been Professor of Dogmatic and Ecumenical Theology at the Theological Faculty in Innsbruck. Recent publications include: *Must There be Scapegoats? Violence and Redemption in the Bible*, San Francisco 1987; *Der wunderbare Tausch. Zur Geschichte und Deutung der Erlösungslehre*, Munich 1986; *Jesus im Heilsdrama. Entwurf einer biblischen Erlösungslehre*, Innsbruck ²1996; *Erbsunde und Heilsdrama. Im Kontext von Evolution, Gentechnologie und Apokalyptik*, Thaur and Münster 1997.

Address: Theologische Fakultät der Leopold-Franzens Universität, Institut für dogmatische und ökumenische Theologie, Universitätsstrasse 4, A-6020 Innsbruck, Austria.

EDWARD SCHILLEBEECKX OP was born on 12 November 1914. He is Emeritus Professor of the Catholic University of Nijmegen. His works are listed in *Bibliography 1936–1997 of Edward Schillebeeckx*, compiled by Ted Schoof OP and Jan van de Westelaken, Baarn 1997.

Address: Mariadal, Oude Kleefsebaan 2, N1–6571, BG Berg en Dal, The Netherlands.

The editors wish to thank the great number of colleagues from the various Advisory Committees who contributed in a most helpful way to the final project.

R. Aguirre	Bilbao	Spain
M. Althaus-Reid	Scotland	UK
G. Dietrich	Madurai	India
F. Elizondo	Madrid	Spain
I. Fischer	Graz	Austria
R. Gibellini	Brescia	Italy
M. Grey	Southampton	UK
M. E. Hunt	Silver Spring	USA
B. van Iersel	Nijmegen	The Netherlands
B. Kern	Mainz	Germany
S. McEvenue	Montreal	Canada
F. W. Menne	Münster	Germany
N. Mette	Münster	Germany
M. A. O'Brien	Box Hill	Australia
E. Pace	Padua	Italy
A. Pieris	Gonawala-Kelaniya	Sri Lanka
P. Richard	San José	Costa Rica
J. Riches	Glasgow	Scotland
R. H. Roberts	Lancaster	UK
S. Schroer	Köniz	Switzerland
A. T. Sanon	Bobo-Dioulasso	Burkina Faso
D. Singles	Lyons	France
R. Strobel	Freiburg	Switzerland

John Templeton Foundation
presents
1998 Science & Religion Course Competition and Workshops

The John Templeton Foundation offers an award program for outstanding courses in science and religion, and a series of workshops on science and religion pedagogy and course development.

Course Competition

The fourth annual Science & Religion Course Competition will award colleges, universities, and seminaries worldwide up to 100 prizes of $10,000 (U.S.) each ($5,000 to the course instructor; $5,000 to the institution) for teaching courses in this interdisciplinary field. *Competition entry deadline is December 1, 1997. Late entry accepted only with enrollment in one of the winter workshops listed below.*

Workshops

Eight workshops instructed by academic leaders teaching in science and religion, will be offered during January, June, and July in the U.S. and England. Winter workshops are *entry-level* training sessions for developing and enhancing science and religion course syllabi and teaching methodologies. Winter workshops are strongly recommended for competition applicants, but are not required. Summer workshops are *advanced-level* training sessions which assume in-depth familiarity with science-religion history and pedagogy issues.

Winter		Summer	
January 3-7, 1998	Tallahassee, Florida	June 11-16, 1998	Berkeley, Calif.
January 7-12, 1998	Oxford, England	June 12-17, 1998	Wenham and
January 15-20, 1998	Berkeley, Calif.		Cambridge, Mass.
		June 19-24, 1998	Chicago, Illinois
		June 29-July 3, 1998	Oxford, England
		July 10-15, 1998	Toronto, Canada

Workshops are limited to 75 participants. A registration fee of U.S. $100 is required to reserve your place. Room and board for the workshops are underwritten by the John Templeton Foundation. *The workshop registration deadlines are December 17, 1997 (winter) and April 15, 1998 (summer). Registration after these deadlines is based on availability.*

For a brochure or complete program application packet and workshop registration materials, contact:
Dr. Robert L. Herrmann, Program Director
Gordon College ▪ 255 Grapevine Road ▪ Wenham, MA 01984
978.927.2306, ext. 4029 (new area code) ▪ Fax: 978.524.3708 ▪ E-mail: herrmann@gordonc.edu
http://www.templeton.org ▪ Reference: CON

CONCILIUM

The Theological Journal of the 1990s

Now available from Orbis Books

Founded in 1965 and published five times a year, *Concilium* is a world-wide journal of theology. Its editors and essayists encompass a veritable 'who's who' of theological scholars. Not only the greatest names in Catholic theology, but also exciting new voices from every part of the world, have written for this unique journal.

Concilium exists to promote theological discussion in the spirit of Vatican II, out of which it was born. It is a catholic journal in the widest sense: rooted firmly in the Catholic heritage, open to other Christian traditions and the world's faiths. Each issue of *Concilium* focusses on a theme of crucial importance and the widest possible concern for our time. With contributions from Asia, Africa, North and South America and Europe, *Concilium* truly reflects the multiple facets of the world church.

Now available from Orbis Books, *Concilium* will continue to focus theological debate and to challenge scholars and students alike.

Concilium Subscription Information - outside North America

Individual Annual Subscription (five issues): £25.00

Institution Annual Subscription (five issues): £35.00

Airmail subscriptions: add £10.00

Individual issues: £8.95 each

New subscribers please return this form:
for a two-year subscription, double the appropriate rate

(for individuals)   £25.00   (1/2 years)   . . . .

(for institutions)   £35.00   (1/2 years)   . . . .

Airmail postage
outside Europe +£10.00   (1/2 years)   . . . .

                                                Total . . . .

I wish to subscribe for one/two years as an individual/institution
(delete as appropriate)

Name/Institution . . . .

Address . . . .

. . . .

. . . .

I enclose a cheque for . . . . payable to SCM Press Ltd

Please charge my Access/Visa/Mastercard no. . . . .

Signature . . . . .Expiry Date . . . .

Please return this form to:
SCM PRESS LTD 9 - 17 St Albans Place   London   N1 0NX